This is ~~~~ ve
cool!
To Ken,

Jim Sweeney
5-21-21

DESTINATION: 8.ZERO

A JOURNAL

JIM SWEENEY

Foreword

This journal was written during my eightieth year. Of course, all birthdays count, but after a certain age I decided only five year and zero-year birthdays were significant!! Yet five years from now, who can guess one's condition? I had neglected writing too long and I needed to write now! Most estimates have the plague known as the novel corona virus (Covid-19) beginning in the USA on January 21, 2020. Not totally cognizant of this existing disaster, I began my journal on January 27, 2020. Who knew a simple exercise in recording everyday thoughts and events would coincide with a pandemic? My wife Joyce and I began our quarantine on March 15, 2020 and I chronicled nearly every day after until my birthday on December 9, 2020 the end of my 80th year. I have taken a ragged, asymmetrical approach to describing this strangest year of most of our lives, but what is normal and balanced about these times? It is an idiosyncratic and highly personal written account. My entries are occasional rants or scattered and sometimes contradictory opinions. I touch on my daily life, friendships and family, politics, personal philosophies, past and current readings and experiences. Even under the pressures of our solitary existence, my intent was always to be honest. However contradictory, my words are what they are, and each reader can judge them as he/she wishes.

Joyce Renneke Sweeney was co-editor, encourager and critic in-chief! This book is dedicated to her.

January 27, 2020

A tad late on starting this New Year, but…

Kobe Bryant and his daughter died in a helicopter crash yesterday with seven other people. Is their loss tragic? It is and it is not; tragic in the young lives unfulfilled, yet we all will die. When and where is to be determined. The only deaths that really matter are those that directly impact you. I mean the loss of one that lessens you and causes you to react to the point of anger, even despair. Do not allow anyone to tell you grief is in your head. It is as physical as a stubbed toe, a paper cut, an exposed nerve in a tooth transferred to your heart. Grieving for yourself is what real loss brings. How could he/she do this to me? Now you see why any other unrelated deaths only get a cursory, obligatory, theoretically expected nod of sympathy from us.

My wife and I feel an immediate sense of urgency in our still new relationship. We are older. We do not have endless time! Paradoxically, at a younger age we had all the time in the world. Kobe and his daughter bear out the fallacious nature of this assumption. But it does seem that way. At our age, "Times winged chariot," and all that passage of time stuff looms large. She and I lack the luxury of screwing things up, then realizing what we did and what we could lose and working to mend it. Pre-emptive actions and words are always in order. We kiss and hug several times a day.

Sadly, Kobe and daughter, it was the unfortunate demise of you both, that partially leads me back to writing.

January 28, 2020

Something I concluded may be so simple, but it is something I would like to share. A few months ago, I had a medical procedure that called for an anesthetic. As they counted down, I noted the time…10:27am. When I came to, forty-three minutes had elapsed. I had been as close to being dead while still breathing. I saw no white light nor heard any voices. My rational mind ceased any activity, my memory disappeared. I longed for nothing, hoped for nothing, recalled nothing. I experienced no envy, no desire, no disappointment, no grief, no happiness, nothing.

I think this is as close to what death is that we can experience. We all will die and all human aspects of us will cease. We will not exist anywhere in any form, except possibly in the memories of the living.

Do not despair, dear Reader. It will lighten up, somewhat!

January 29, 2020

I am not superstitious nor religious in any traditional sense. At best, I try to maintain a spiritual life. I hesitate to say I believe in karma because it seems so random, but it does appear on occasion and I experienced it in back to back days.

The first incident occurred yesterday. I drove to my 7-11 and parked at the entry. A young girl was by the door. She could have been sixteen or twenty. She sat against the store wall with a duffel bag behind her. I got out of my car, glanced at her, and said nothing. I made my purchase and left. She was still there; this was no kid from the affluent high school just behind the store. I asked her if she was all right. She nodded no, near tears.

"Something's wrong," I said. A garbled response: "I came to Florida with a boy. I need a bus ticket to Allentown, PA." "How much have you got?" Not enough, so I gave her a twenty. I told her to get something to eat and she said someone had bought her a hot dog. Before I left, a young man left the store, entered his car next to mine, then got out and handed her some change. She thanked him and me too when I drove away. She was no grifter, possibly a runaway. She was a decent looking kid, but she needed everything. In the past in Skokie I would have taken her home. Jerri Rae would have had her showered, laundered her clothes and fed her within an hour. The times have changed all that.

Just outside of the 7-11 parking lot a Pinellas County deputy was giving a ticket to a high school girl. She drove an expensive car. I waited until he was done. "Officer, there's a kid over there who needs some help." "Where?" "In front of the store." He got in his squad car and headed that way. I hoped he would find a runaway shelter for her to spend the night. Everyone laughs when we say it gets cold in Florida. Try spending a night outside in 40 degrees! Some bastards might offer her "shelter," too.

I hate how things are. After thirty-seven years of teaching and taking care of kids and never worrying about "consequences," I limited myself to doing a perfunctory bit for this girl. I should have done more.

January 30, 2020

Part two...Karma rears its' lovely head. The next day I rode my bike from my house. As I turned a corner, the largest Mayflower moving van I ever saw was parked with its' driver idling the engine. Two young black men and an older white guy stood by the truck talking. I noted them because they were in front of a friend's house. But it was the house next door with the "contract pending" sign that had been emptied and loaded. Somebody said: "How's it going? "Good." Kept riding around another corner, same street. Heard the big van clash into gear and knew it was coming. I decided to swing up a driveway and ride the side-walk until it passed. When it did, I went to exit at the next driveway, but I came too close to the lawn. My bike hit a deep cutaway around a watering pop-up, yanked the front wheel to the left and put me on the ground. I scraped my left hand and landed hard on my left shoulder.

A car stopped and the two young guys I had just seen jumped out. "you ok, man?" "Can you help me up?" I am 6:2, 240 with knees like glass. The bigger one reached down with both hands, grabbed my arms above each elbow and had me on my feet in an instant! We are talking dead weight! The smaller guy had his arm around my waist and helped me into his car. They were cousins...Darius and David. Darius drove me home and David walked the bike as the chain had come off. They were following the van, which they had just loaded, to Jupiter, FL to unload it when they saw me go down.

Joyce came out to meet them. David was not leaving until he got the chain on right and put the bike in the garage. We gave them cokes and money for some lunch. I will skip a rant over the burden they bore being black in America or the white man's guilt and lack of retribution. Let me just say they were kindness personified and the world and me is better off with them in it.

January 31, 2020

My favorite day/night of the year! Even better than Christmas Eve or my birthday! I go to bed tonight and wake up financially improved tomorrow!

February 1, 2020

We secured in my last teacher strike in 1996 enhanced retirement benefits for ourselves and ultimately for many Illinois teachers if they would pledge to retire in return for salary bumps in their final years. The 3% annual retirement raise re-occurs every 2/1 for hundreds of District 219 retired teachers and thousands more Illinois retired teachers. Because of the previously described enhanced benefits, the raise takes on a more significant meaning. I am proud to be a part of this achievement and it was a difficult part I played. But to think how many people live more comfortably today because of our courage warms my old heart! Called Jim Doherty and suggested a celebration of this event in 2021… the 25th year anniversary!

February 2, 2020

Not much to report…we decided to buy a car (an indulgent toy!) of which I will tell you later. Bargained half-heartedly with the lady owner/manager of Alpha Auto Traders. She called her husband/co-owner and he okayed a $200 drop in price. Used car…got a replaced windshield wiper and a free scan that showed no serious problems. New convertible top and new tires. Put another $200 down to hold it for a day. We enjoyed our trial drive through Tampa's Forest Hills around Babe Zaharias Golf Course.

February 3 and 4, 2020

Eyes it, tries it, buys it!!! We spent the morning at my insurance agency. My agent friend Linda slow walked us through the addition of the car and Joyce to the policy as a driver. It is a 2004 Mercedes Benz CLK 500 with 90000 miles on it. Exterior black in no ding condition, interior tan with a couple of minor rips and worn spots. Cost…cheap! We both threw in on the purchase price so that Joyce could be on the title. Anything happens, the car is hers.

It is so much fun to drive and, even at sixteen years, it has features we just heard of with our "real" cars. You adjust your seat and the wing mirrors adjust! Got seat heaters…great in Florida!!! I am ashamed to say I could hardly wait to get it home to one up my teenage neighbor, Michael. He is a great kid who got a fire engine red Camaro on his 16th birthday. He was impressed!

I told Joyce we were like Seinfeld's parents in Florida. Jerry gave them a Caddy and insisted they not go to the early bird dinner. Their condo friends called them Mr. and Mrs. Got Rocks!!!

Al Zammit loved it and typically only wanted to know the price. Bob Murray asked if I had won the lottery! My garbage man Ken who always calls me "young man," said, "you will look great with the wind blowing through your hair." I am completely bald.

February 5, 2020

This is an important day in my personal history, and it grows more significant as the years pass. After several months of pondering, reading, discussing and praying, I entered the Christian Brothers, a Catholic teaching order, on this date 57 years ago in 1963. My parents drove me from our home in Lima, OH to the nearest large airport in Dayton, OH. It was my first flight. I flew to St. Louis, then by car to the monastery in Glencoe, MO. I was 22.

How did all of this come about? I still ask myself. Was I simply trying to get out of a job that I hated six months after graduation? Was I seeking a secure area in which to escape? Was I really compelled to a life of religious service or did the novelty of my announcement to family and friends so intrigue me? Probably, aspects of all these speculations came into play. I remained in this life for six years and four months under the vows of poverty, chastity and obedience. I learned to teach in Memphis, TN and Wichita, KS. I earned a master's degree in English literature, made many dear secular friends, lived with and grew very fond of many of the men I called Brother and chose to leave before final vows. The effects of these years color my existence to this day in some good ways and one or two ways that needed to be overcome.

February 6, 2020

Replaced my propane tank, watered my lawns, went to the produce store, wrote in my journal, rode my bike, worked out, read, did laundry and cooked dinner. Not much else to do!

February 9, 2020

Yesterday I set my personal best on the f/x elliptical machine. 3.20 miles, 503 calories, done in 47 minutes. Will increase this to one hour. As I said to Joyce: "I'm down to my last competition…myself."

My cousin Barbra Price, whose mom was my Aunt Ann Eisel, was 80 on 2/7 or 2/8. She was my childhood tomboy buddy and a practiced buffer between my sister and me. As mentioned, I will be eighty in December of 2020. My sister is 81, 82 in May. The Eisel genes are potent, not so the Sweeney's. My mom, Margaret Eisel, lived to be 101 years and a couple of months. My Aunt Alice Eisel Wagner died at 96. My Aunt Ann Eisel Price lived until 95. Their father, Thomas Eisel, died at 93. The boys did not fare so well. Tom Jr. at 70 of natural causes, and Art at 41, mysteriously. More like their mother, Nell, who died relatively young at 56.

Joyce and I are 77 and 79, respectively. We are in good health and extremely immature. We think we are young!!!

My Aunt Ann Eisel was the only person in my life who loved me unconditionally!!!

In "A Farewell to Arms," Hemingway describes the main character's disillusionment and existential angst with the war by having him discard all lofty words like *truth, patriotism, integrity, flag, bravery* and *courage*...he only names places, and peoples' names and weapons' nomenclature. So too do I feel about the time I spent in the Christian Brothers Teaching Order. I do recall the theological studies, the meditation practice, the prayers, the aloneness, the spiritual aridity and the vows and the Rule. I absorbed these for a year and more in the monastery. Then I was thrown into teaching and communal living trying to deal with socialization, students, parents and outside friendships. All the trappings were peeled away and all the lofty concepts I had learned became temporarily meaningless. Only the essence of service remained.

Just recently I received a list of the dates of brothers who died in the Order. January 1 through December 31, year by year since the beginning of the 20th century. The names of many I loved came back to me in a tsunami of recollection. And with them came the place names: Glencoe, MO, the Novitiate, Chicago, Lewis College in Lockport IL. Memphis, TN, the Scholasticate, Christian Brothers' College, Christian Brothers' Academy and Memphis State University, Bishop Carroll HS in Wichita, KS.

February 10, 2020

From above....Names: John Dubois, Tom Davis, Tom Wojac, Roger Seklecky, Steve O'Malley, Joel Carr, Lefty Dominic, Phil Lynch, Vic Moeller, Stan Brostowski, Rod Beerman, Ted Lorenz, "Markey" Marcus, Kevin Convey, Jim Friehaut, Levian Powers, George Carney, Jet Set John, Connie Sullivan, "The Jaw" John Coakley, Jack Doody, Luke Grande (my mentor), Jim Cunningham, Kansas City Bernard, Patti and Joan Averwater, Larry, Anna Pellegrini, Nell Sharp, Fran Martin, Carol Sadler, Myles and Sherry Finnegan, The Carney brothers, Joe and Monica Flynn, Paul Dugan (later Lt. Governor of Kansas).

Watching the political news and checking my Google assures me that I am living in an alien, alternate universe.

Bernie Sanders is the guy in the Angry Orchard Cider television ads. He is always hot, even in a cool medium like TV that abhors rants. He has no wit, no smiles, no self-deprecation. To him life's problems are an onerous burden that must be crushed, not finessed. He is never not mad. Have a beer with him? Not on your life! He will throw it in your face if you disagree with him. With his white hair flying around like a demented version of actor Christopher Lloyd, he seems only happy when he loses so he can keep on hammering his causes without ever having to solve them. Who does not want what he wants? At what cost can all these free things be achieved? Sorry, Bernie, hate us for what we are not, not Finns, Swedes, Danes or Norwegians. We are a capitalist country, whether you or I like it. You have never governed apart from being mayor of Burlington, VT. One way or another, you will play a big part in returning Trump to office either by running and losing or watching your folks withhold 12% of their votes from another nominee like they did last time.

February 12, 2020

Off to Chicago June 17 to the 22nd. Graduation celebrations for Jordan, James and Julian. Just confirmed our reservation at the Country Inn and Suites in Gurnee for the duration.

Owen Faulhaber's birthday today. Jordan's long-time boyfriend with whom she recently broke up. Loved the kid, and…wished him a happy birthday, anyway, on Facebook.

3.43 miles…535 calories…50 minutes Woot! A personal best on the f/x machine!

Kris Kristofferson got a letter from his mom disowning him for leaving his army career to be a song writer. He showed it to his producer, who said: "Nothing like a letter from home." It reminded me of my mother writing me that the family would never attend my wedding to Jerri Rae after my divorce from Pam. That hurt but I ignored it. I immediately wrote back, thanked them for the letter, and proceeded to cheerfully detail our wedding plans.

Willie Nelson said that Kris was the greatest songwriter ever. Larry Gatlin said he was better than Johnny Mercer! "All the words have always been there, but nobody strung them together like Kris."

"Bless us and save us, said Mrs. O'Davis…Joy, Joy, said Mrs. Malloy!" Quote from Jack Albertson's character in "The Subject was Roses," the filmed version of the Broadway play that was Martin Sheen's first movie role, 56 years ago.

February 14, 2020

Valentine's Day with my honey. Exchanged cards and I got a cool Mercedes Benz key fob for the new (used) car's ignition key. Joyce got nothing. My dumb gift is not here so I stuck the ad for it on FB in her card! Dinner at the new Water Oak Grill in Safety Harbor. Excellent meal...took an uber there and back. Felt like a confessional therapist as both drivers unloaded their feelings. St. Joyce kept them going!

February 15, 2020

Where do the days go? Cami and the kids arrive at 8:30 tonight. First plane ride for Owen and Avery! Been grocery shopping, getting wine for Cam (who'll need it!") cleaning the deck and heating the pool. Got tickets for Bush Gardens for all day Monday. Emmy gets to ride from the airport in the convertible with her idol, Miss Joyce. Cannot fit everyone in the Jeep. So, two cars must go to the airport. Going to try to take Emmy to an old shopping center parking lot to teach her how to drive. Did the same thing with my girls in Michigan at a younger age. Hope she will go with me.

Surprise visit this morning from Nina Gildersleeve, our former golf pro, and a dear friend. Back in Florida on business and she wanted to meet Joyce and get a hug from the Sweenman! Lives in Medina, OH with her partner, Molly Sureck, who I love too. Made my day! Ran into Dave Semrau at Publix, too. An old friend from Detroit.

February 16 to 18, 2020

They landed! So much to do! We took Emmy to a newly constructed road with only a few new houses about a quarter mile away and let her drive! She is 14 and did a decent job with her right foot…gas, brake, gas, brake! I think she texted everyone she knew." I can drive!" Grilled cheese toast with sliced tomatoes… grilled dogs for the younger guys, mac and cheese and chopped salad for the 14 years old vegan. Avery is the best. Such a smart nine years old. Loves to dance, read and swim. Stops every now and then to give me a hug. Insatiable curiosity! Tried to explain Schrodinger's Cat experiment to her. "Write it down…I'll take it to my teacher." She reads some book editions with terrific illustrations…Just like I read Classic Comics! Owen…a still developing story…going to be a sports machine! They liked Busch Gardens which is a local treasure! Total visit cost?--- worth every penny! Still tired and Joyce has a bad cold and cough!

February 20, 2020

The final (?) Democrat debate debacle was last night. I am perplexed and disappointed and doubting our chances to beat Trump. The candidates did a wholesale savaging of Mike Bloomberg. Two white men, a young man, two women of the Senate trashed the guy for every PC violation of his life, his massive wealth, his mega-successful business creation and his three term stint as mayor of NYC. Not exactly a circular firing squad, though a few rounds landed on varying targets, but rather a verbal assault on MB which I hope is not fatal. He should have been more prepared and engaged, but he chose to remain above it to his chagrin.

New personal best on the f/x elliptical…3.5 miles, 551 calories in 51 minutes.

February 21, 2020

So glad little Joyce is coughing less and feeling somewhat better. It has been a rough two days and nights. Going to make her a special dinner tonight.

February 26, 2020

Special Dinner tomorrow night. Excited about resumption of Tai Chi tomorrow with Master Kelly! Personal best on the f/x elliptical yesterday. 4.03 miles…625 calories…one hour!!!! Took the day off!

No booze tonight! Did some calculations today…Starting in March of 2014, just after Jerri's passing and running until Jordan's and James' graduation in June, I have and will have given away quite a bit of post taxes cash. Not a penny to a church or an organized charity. Every dollar has gone to individuals who desperately needed something. The Sweeney Foundation exists in my head! Never took a single tax deduction, either.

Dinner went well…Ribeye was perfect! First shot at chunky garlic mashed potatoes. Did not quite get the roasted garlic right. Better next time. Second night without booze. Day at a time.

February 29, 2020

Hic sunt dracones. "Here be dragons." Written at the point on the globe where the world ends. Also, dragons rise out of the sea at the edge of the world on flat world maps.

March 1, 2020

"March comes in like a lion a-kickin' up the water in the Bay!" (*Carousel)* 44 degrees…freezing!

A couple of days ago an older gentleman came into the Zone health club. He was tall, about 6:3 and razor thin with a well-coiffed head of white hair, nice jeans, sport shirt and the required NBs. I was on my f/x elliptical and he went to a treadmill directly in front of me. "You got my back?" "Definitely." Hip old dude!

Later we spoke again. The usual "looking good, working hard" exchange. Your name? "Richard," he said. "Name's Jim, how old are you?" ninety-one. "Good for you." My "I'll be 80 my next birthday," paled into insignificance. "My wife will be 91 in two months," Richard proudly announced. I went to the door and got a waiting Joyce to meet this gentleman.

Introductions over, Richard ask where we were from. He was from Philadelphia, "lived across the street from the Liberty Bell!" "My parents and I had just moved to Philly and some older boys were teaching me how to play football in the park. They sent me out for a pass and there she was, sitting on the grass, the prettiest girl, ever. I stopped and stared at her and forgot to catch the ball. They all yelled but I didn't care."

"Started first grade and she was again sitting right by me, so blond her family called her 'snowball.' We have been together ever since. I love talking to young people."

About seventy-one years of being married is a great achievement but being married to your first grade girlfriend is a grand slam, hat trick, OT three pointer combined!

Here we are, Joyce and me, three years and seven months together and 14 months married today, pinching ourselves each day over our good fortune.

March 7, 2020

My wife of nearly 37 years, Jerri Rae, died on this day in 2014 in Countryside Hospital. I was not with her. Her lungs were seriously compromised by cancer and she was breathing through a full face mask. The protocol was to keep reducing the mask size down to where she could breath on her own. This was not working and, according to her living will, she could not be artificially kept alive for an indeterminate time. My daughters and I knew this and tried to come to grips with the fact that her time was at hand. Late in her last day she began to struggle fiercely with the mask. I tried to hold her hands down. Her nurse rushed in and told me I was upsetting her and I should leave the room. I went to the waiting area at the end of the hall. The "stat" alarm went off and I saw people rushing carts into the room. I hurried there but the door was closed and I could not get in. She passed in a few minutes. My daughters were here and had been with her earlier, but we did not get to say goodbye and it haunts us to this day.

March 8, 2020

Where have the last seven days gone? James' birthday is past, Julia's coming as well as Cam's. Taxes are done. Thank you, Gary Moore, tax man. Wallpaper stripped in the middle guest bathroom, tiles all bought, fixtures to be delivered this week…Defco Tile ready to start.

Jill and Mike coming Thursday, always welcome guests.

Biden is surging and Bernie (maybe?) on the ropes. Field cleared, but much disputation unresolved. Gender bias looming large and possibly coming to a head. Dems, per usual and rightly so, bring the ugly stuff to the front. But I feel the Bernie gang are Donner Partying the opposition who happen to be democrats, too. Why is getting this joker Trump out not our priority? We democrats have a history of screw ups, and that is a fact. Please, all of us pull together and keep the enemy in mind.

I am temporarily off FB, politically. Too many younger, smarter people going after this geezer's comments. I am getting into too many rants. I cannot seem to grasp so many current facts or so many democrat establishment's "errors and betrayals." I am the beneficiary of so much good after so many strikes and such tough bargaining and union solidarity even though that appears to many these days to be ancient history. Grateful is one thing, a tad out of touch, another.

Xavier cannot be in the NCAA field of 68 and they are not. What a frustrating season! For the first time, I am even down on Travis Steele. How can you not get a team ready for the final game?

Talked to Avery a couple of nights ago. Ask her if she mentioned Schrodinger's Cat to her teacher. Said she did. Teacher said maybe talk about it after we finish this material. Asked A. if she believed her? Nope, she replied. Did not think so, either.

March 9, 2020

My friend John Mascari is going to get his first treatment on 3/19. He is getting a dose of something to attack the cancer in his bladder…not radiation nor chemo.

March 15, 2020

DAY 1

It begins. This plague has grabbed our full attention. We are at quarantine one!

March 16, 2020

DAY 2

Will this ever end? Going crazy! (kidding)

March 17, 2020

St. Patrick's Day…DAY 3

Eight weeks into the plague, officially noted as beginning January 21, 2020…we are self-sequestered for our third day.

March 18, 2020

DAY 4

Day four and we are doing fine. Cannot think of who I would rather be locked up with than Joyce. This morning I was Jimmy, the forager/provider! Publix had no potatoes, bread, onions or tp. But I got pasta and meatballs, one white onion, Kleenex and freezer bags. Then the coup of the week! The produce market on Tarpon Springs Road. Wow!!! A giant artichoke, tomatoes, baking potatoes, La Segunda bread and ravioli. The Mrs. cleaned the bathroom, but I hunted provender. Never had a hobby in my life, but cooking is my first crack at one. Have eaten great food all around the world. I took an on-line chef's course and ended up buying the whole course for day to day reference.

Rode my bike; Joyce took a walk. We are coping nicely…planning simple meals, working out, swimming and reading. Mapping out movies on all the cables. Kind of made a pact on CNN and MSNBC. I watch it for about a half hour early…Joyce does too after she gets up. Too depressing sitting in front of it for long periods of time. Still addicted to FB.

Keeping in touch with the girls, my Cait, Cam and Joyce's Lisa and Jill.

March 22, 2020

DAY 8

Day 8 of self-quarantine. We take our temperatures every morning as we think this is the first discernible symptom. They are normal for both. Joyce takes over the cooking with beef bourguignon for dinner. I did shrimp creole last night. I avoid watching much virus tv. Know all the warnings, epicenters, and Florida fuckups! We just want to avoid trump's obnoxious self. Did learn a new word yesterday used by a writer describing Trump's pressers...mephitic! Means a foul, noxious smell that would emit from the opening cut of a trump autopsy!

March 23, 2020

DAY 9

Beef Bourguignon was great last night. Two rich meals in a row...eating light today. Both of our temps are normal. Why will the President not activate the full power of the Emergency Act? States and other states and the Fed are competing for prices on needed goods. Why is there no Federal (national) coordination? Continual rumbling among progressives about withholding a vote from Biden. One Chicago joker posted on FB "Is Joe Biden dead?" I hope they figure out a way to hold each remaining primary and I hope Bernie runs until every vote is counted and loses them all. Do not know if there will be a convention or another candidate, possibly Cuomo, emerging. Then the progressives can work their magic! They can withhold a vote for Joe, write in someone else or just flat out vote for Trump. Then they can have four full years to refine their positions and determine their standard bearer, if we are still here, Joyce and I will be fine.

March 24, 2020

DAY 10

Day 10 for us inside. This is the first night of take-out from a favorite restaurant. Got to support them. Is Dr. Fauci gone? He is the only adult in the room! The daily pressers are becoming the SNL acts of the next week. "soon, pretty soon, we'll see, incredible, Debbie." Reminds me of remedial classes I taught. If I heard a kid struggling to read aloud, I would rescue him from embarrassment. Someone should do that for Trump. No-lips Pence…stuck on Trump's ass.

March 25, 2020

DAY 11

Trying to avoid rants…but those press updates!!! Yikes! First half Trump… pure fiction (lies and ignorant claims), second half…dire truths from the scientists. Of course, Pence's usual fawning and ass kissing. The latest: we will be in churches together, nationwide, on Easter Sunday, says the non-Christian, non-anything, poster child for evil President! All people with half a brain cell should be frightened and outraged.

March 28, 2020

DAY 14

Day 14…Les Hunter RIP. Les starred on the 1963 Loyola Ramblers NCAA championship team. He was the center who could rebound and whip the ball out to start a fast break. This was a time when two blacks on the floor at the same time was verboten. Loyola made a statement by starting four. Racism was rampant,

But these guys played through it and upset Cincinnati who had beaten a powerful Ohio State in the 1962 NCAA championship. I had entered the Christian Brothers Monastery in Glencoe, MO, as previously mentioned, on February 5, 1963. About a month and a half into it, I caught a cold. Brother John, sub director, told me to stay in bed that next morning. I slept in and was still in bed at 2:00pm. Knock on my door. Brother Director with a small radio. "I thought you might want to listen to the Loyola game." I had graduated from Xavier in '62. He may have mistakenly thought Loyola. It was one of the kindest gestures anyone has ever shown me. Spent the historic afternoon with Les Hunter, Egan, Roush, Harkrader, Coach Ireland and all others. What a game! What a win for Loyola!

March 28.

(continued)

Made the world's biggest meatloaf along with mashed potatoes and peas. Yum!
Bought my honey flowers.

March 29. 2020

DAY 15

I am about as much at peace as I have ever been. We literally have turned off the
tv. All we see and hear are the manic rants of trump and rising covid numbers.
We stay in except for groceries and booze. Up in the morning to check temps and
do the breathing exercise. So far, fine. No symptoms. Joyce walks. I do my combination of stationary bike, heavy bag and bands in the garage. Reading three
books concurrently and keeping in touch with a sick friend and my many viral
friends and former students on FB. Cocktails at 5:00, 5:30 and I make dinner.
Talk to the girls frequently. Will do a zoom birthday party tonight for Owen's
birthday. Joyce will try to split screen with Caitlen's gang, too. Do not ask me
how! This quarantine will not last forever or maybe it will!

March 30, 2020

DAY 16

Figured Joyce has had enough meatloaf. Made her a surprise dinner…plum tomatoes with garlic and parmesan, carrots, little Yukon potatoes, onions and asparagus. All roasted in olive oil and sea salt. Delish! Got my IRA money released from E-Trade and safe in my money market. We have cleaned out the garage! A lot of little kid stuff gone…no more little ones, except for sweet Julia who calls me and Joyce simply PappaJoyce! Things are sinking in---no college graduation for Jordie, a once in a lifetime event, no middle school graduation for James, maybe no summer camp for Emmy. Life has delivered them a butt kick early on. Hope we can still get together in June.

March 31, 2020

DAY 17

Hauled all the garage cleaning junk to the curb for my garbage boys, Carey and Ken. A Jackson for each of them…tip them all…waiters, waitresses, janitors, delivery folk, garbage guys, lawn guys, pool guys. Need them all. Got to admit, just a bit down in the dumps. No June visit with the guys in Gurnee for a graduation party, no wedding for CP and Angela, no Ft. Myers family vacation in June/July. A bit of self-pity is in order. Cannot "guarantee" the future like I used to do. Running out of years. OK, cut the crap, ENOUGH!

April 1, 2020

DAY 18

What a Fool's Day!

April 2, 2020

DAY 19

Fighting off a bout of lassitude…one day at a time is the only answer. Deleted the FB post about Pete Sakas' passing. It was accurate and maybe even needed, but it seemed like a bit of self-aggrandizing to me. I more knew of him than knew him, but he is the first person who has died in my circle of acquaintances. For the first time in my life, something in the realm of physical well-being is frightening me. Because of my age and asthma, I am a bit concerned. Trying to take especial care. God love my Joycie. Get back to cooking, working out, taking rides and talking to the kids. Have temporarily lost interest in FB. Hate Trump just as much, now Governor DeSantis, his favorite puppet. But takes too much energy. Focus positive.

Painter is finishing the guest bathroom tomorrow. Glass shower doors to follow.

April 6, 2020

DAY 23

Am into the mask and gloves 100%. Mask is a reconstituted airline sleeping mask and my gloves are two spiffy, brand new white Titleist gloves with fancy ball markers attached. Went to Publix and found about half the shoppers ignoring everything...no mask, gloves or distancing. Fuck them. Let them die but not me or Joyce. Talked to my brother who is borderline concerned...no mask, gloves, plays golf and visits friends who, as Dr. Tom insists, "are not sick." Go figure!

OK...This is a rehearsal FB piece. I will employ my eloquent yet understated composition style. I hate President Trump and I hope he loses in November. Even though Joe Biden is not the strongest candidate, he will get our vote and that is about as much as we can do. With the current state of life as it is for my wife and me, the election is on the distant horizon. If, at our age, we can get through this plague, that is exacerbated by this bumbling, incompetent, arrogant, lying president, without dying, we will be happy. If Trump wins because angry, righteous democrats write-in names, vote only down ballot or refuse to vote at all over some alleged DNC grievance, so be it. As Johnny Friendly said in "On the Waterfront," "You want him? You got him!" You part-time blue voters will own him. See how much of your progressive agenda gets advanced in the next four years! So much for any American institutions Trump has not yet destroyed. Quarantining is not all that bad. Much bullshit has been eliminated from our lives in just a few weeks. Good training for more Trump in our future! Speaking only for ourselves, we can do it indefinitely!

April 7, 2020

DAY24

Making a contact/computer list of usernames, passwords, phone #s, and locations of documents for the kids.

April 8, 2020

DAY 25

We found out yesterday that our lawyer had died on February 15. We were not important clients who had to be notified immediately. He was one of the most intelligent, likeable and interesting persons I have ever met. Joyce was looking up his phone # online because she could not find his card and inadvertently came across his obituary. He might have died of a heart attack…I am not sure… but no words referenced the virus. However, his sudden death at 59 shocked me and underscored the absurdity of our existence, particularly because of this virus. Everyone is going to die! Why was I shocked? The fact that this reality is so hard to understand and accept is what is absurd. History and Camus in *La Peste* remind us that plagues appear and reappear. A plague is death in exaggerated numbers. Absurdity can be defined as that which is not known nor can be explained, even when we can formulate the questions. What is even more absurd is the notion that we will revert to some previous state when this subsides as if the virus never happened and deaths will go back to being "normal." Death is the plague and our very existence speaks to its omnipresence.

April 9, 2020

DAY 27 (Holy Thursday)

I always wondered about the meaning of "Maundy Thursday?" To me it was always Holy Thursday but wasn't the whole week Holy Week? Maundy is an Anglo-French word for "commandment," derived from the Latin word "mandatum" which tangentially means the same...to mandate or command. And what was this command? "To love one another..." But that came at the end of a long, harrowing day for Jesus.

Currently, the mass commemorating the Last Supper is held at sundown of Passover. The blessing of holy oils occurs, as well as the establishment of the priesthood with the washing of feet. Just as Christ did with his apostles, the first priests. Then the Blessed Sacrament is placed on the altar to be adored throughout the night. Jesus went to the Garden to pray and the Roman Soldiers came to arrest him. Peter cut the ear of one and Jesus rebuked him. Judas, ridden with guilt, slunk away to hang himself. The others slept through it all. One tough night but it will only get worse...

April 10, 2020

DAY 28

Not so Good Friday

Altar stripped, tabernacle door left open, no Eucharist, sanctuary candle blown out, hangings removed, everything decked in purple, Passion of Christ reenacted in the Stations of the Cross. Silent prayer from 12:00 noon until 3:00pm. Unfair trial, unnecessary flogging, crucifixion (punishment for outlaws) stabbed in the side, slow, painful death. Fear and chaos among the faithful. The rock bottom has been reached!

April 11, 2020

DAY 29

Holy Saturday

We suspend everything in the liturgy now. Then, sadness and holding of breath. What is going to happen to this nascent community? Keeping watch at the tomb. Something big is coming!!! But what?

April 12, 2020

Easter Sunday...DAY 30 (He is risen again!)

US death toll passes Italy! We are at 20000! Three friends dead in Illinois, Dave Schusteff, Pete Sakas and Bill Richardson. Getting close to home! Not despairing but wondering...hoping family and friends are OK. Hating people who fail to get it, do not care or are just stupid. No mask, no gloves, no distancing. Jeez!

Took a long drive---top down! Campbell Causeway to the Kennedy to Bayshore Dr. to Ballast Point and back by way of MacDill AFB, Central Command (Cent Com) for all our military actions.

April 13, 2020

DAY 31

We visited the Hudson Grotto, the site of my second checkout scuba dive in 2005 for my PADI certification. Friendly dive guy let us walk over to the pool, which is a prehistoric sinkhole, 155 feet deep and maybe 30000 years old, according to some FSU scientists. One can dive down into an underground river via a cave. Not me! Pitch black in there! Drove to Hudson Beach than back to New Port Richey and checked out the houses on the Pithlachascotee River.

We pretty much decided that Q will last until the end of May then all hell will break loose if re-entry into the economy is not done intelligently and incrementally. Yep, right! When pigs fly!

Checking out.

April 14, 2020

DAY 32

Uncle Crazy announces that he has power over all of states and he will tell us when we are to go back to work and to school. Constitutional crisis looming. Cuomo organizing NY, PA, DEL. CONN, NJ and little Rhode Island. Governor Newsome doing the same with CA, OR and WA. Talk about a collision course!

Read, biked, wrote, swam. Made sausage and ravioli for dinner.

April 15, 2020

DAY 33

As usual, Uncle Crazy backed down! Now it is all on the Governors! One contradiction/lie after another from this guy!

A quote from Camus: "Life is a hospice, never a hospital." "The universe is indifferent; it is neither moral nor evil." The plague (novel coronavirus) is a sickness, but allegorically, symbolically and metaphorically it is the existence of sudden, random death to which we are all subject.

We foolishly plan, set alarms for the morning, expect and hope for a future which may or may not happen. In our present situation, there is no future. If, however, this plague ceases, we will go right back to the past and be caught totally unaware again. Dinner tonight from Mamma Maria's.

April 16, 2020

DAY 34

Trump has officially backed down! As the unemployment rises, his election grows in jeopardy. So, he has thrown it back on the governors when to open. Some gibberish about 14 days of no new cases but no word about testing. Obviously, the states cannot afford to do it, not to mention their lack of technical help.

I hope the CA team and the NY team can pull something off.

A sad call from Cam late yesterday afternoon elicited some angry words from me to my granddaughter Emmy that I later regretted. I will listen to any problem, but lately I am often stumped for answers.

April 17, 2020

DAY 35

Playing some catch-up. Home all day and still cannot get everything done. Talk about a goofy situation. Between meal planning, some in-store shopping, reading, writing, Spanish lessons, FB postings, and working out, I am always behind. I told Joyce that I should feel guilty for not feeling bad being quarantined. In fact, my latest FB post advocates staying in at least two weeks after any state opens. Let the crazies test the water, absorb the first inevitable resurge of coronavirus, and keep ourselves safe. There is nothing that beats the fact of being old. There is little we have not done or need to do.

April 18, 2020

DAY 36

Finally, a hard rain. Knocks down the pollen for us allergy guys. My grass has never looked better. Cool and grey all day. New masks for us made in Tampa. Dinner was Friday night's take out from Sip85. One of our favorite menu items that we did not eat immediately because we backed up the gumbo and had to eat the fresh shrimp…Sip85's charcuterie was a day later. Went inside the door of the restaurant and saw one of our favorites, Angie, as always behind the bar. She asked about my "honey bunny," and I was delighted to give her a $20 tip on a $21.00 bill. She is a cutie and she made me realize that I missed outside contact more than I thought. And that brings me to Joyce. I love her so much and would die without her. We marvel at the fact that there is never a harsh word between us. We can pass an entire afternoon on one topic…our dads, for example, and how in our old age we realize how much we loved our parents and how good they were to us. We seldom pass each other without a kiss, hug or touch. The beauty is in our newness with each other. No forty or fifty years of grievances. Lucky is not word enough for us. Never finish this topic.

April 19, 2020

DAY 37

The gumbo…a lot of chopping of onion, garlic, celery, green peppers (the trinity in NOLA talk) chicken and andouille sausage plus the shrimp and okra. Piece de resistance…finally made a dark roux!!! Took pictures of it and made sure John "NOLA Nunu" Zomot saw them on FB. Forty minutes of nonstop stirring! Little flour here, more oil there! It was delicious. Did nothing else but prep for it after we came back from our ride.

April 20, 2020

DAY 38

It is still early in the day. Temps taken…plus check our blood to oxygen ratios. Besides how you feel, these are sure gauges of your health status. We are well within temp range, always below 98.6. Not always sure of the testing question and what negative really means. Is everyone getting tested showing the symptoms? Unless you pay for it yourself, you must have something from a doctor that certifies symptoms to be tested. So, if you test negative, all that means is you still can get it…or maybe you had it and are over it.

April 21, 2020

DAY 39

Recommended a monumental article from The Atlantic entitled "Our Pandemic Summer," on FB. Written on 4/14/2020. It comes down to the fact that we face a national crisis led by an ill-prepared and incompetent fool. If we get out of this alive it will not be to the credit of this dolt, except, of course, he will credit himself!

I can handle this Q. I Look to Hugh Hefner for my inspiration. Forty years and never left the house…always a smile on his face. I am smiling, too, at the one lady with whom I want to be.

Grocery shopping to make chicken salad. As Southern Living magazine states: "Every Southern girl has her own special chicken salad recipe!"

April 22, 2020

DAY 40!!!!!!

The word quarantine is derived from the Latin root quaranta or forty.

#Forty, in Hebraic and Aramaic, was a common linguistic and hyperbolic numerical to add importance and weight to a statement. Frequently used by the unknown writers of the Scripture to emphasize persons and events…not to be taken literally. It means not just a numerical amount but a "long, long time." Lent, Advent, time spent in the desert by Jesus, John and other prophets.

OK, we have served our time, biblically speaking, as of today!!!

One man's Facebook response to hoarders of toilet paper, hand sanitizers, bleach and gloves:

Fuck off

Fuck off as far as you can see

When you come to a fence bearing a sign that reads

"No more fucking off beyond this point,"

Jump the fence, dream the impossible dream,

And keep fucking off forever.

You disgust me! (courtesy of Dave Lewis)

A tip of the hat to Jack, Stephen King's fictional character, who voluntarily quarantined himself, his wife and son in "The Shining: "All work and no play makes Jack a dull boy, All work and no play makes Jack a dull boy, All work and no play…"

April 23, 2020

DAY 41

House cleaning. Joyce on the sweeper…me cycling the lawn rotors and doing the wash. Looking forward to making meatballs and spaghetti tonight. News getting grimmer and grimmer. Georgia newest covid-19 nut case state. Tattoo parlors open tomorrow. Wonder if Georgians would grasp a sign I spotted in Louisville: "Tattoos done while you wait!!" Governor of Georgia just found out that the virus was transmitted person to person and was stupid enough to announce his new-found wisdom to the public!

Corona deniers first in the pool! Very fond of much of Georgia, but will they ever get over their debtor colony syndrome?

April 24, 2020

DAY 42

The maniac wants us to stick ultra-violet probes up our rear ends and then intravenously drip some Lysol or Clorox into our veins to kill Covid-19. Really, no further comment needed.

Last night's meat balls were delicious. About a pound and one half of chuck, one egg, generous dollop of Worcester sauce, parsley flakes, salt/pepper, onion and oats. Thirty minutes at 420 degrees and another thirty in my homemade pasta sauce.

Not much for Covid-19 theories, but Joyce and I think there is a possibility that we might have had it in December and February. In December of 2019, Cam and Emmy came down for three days. Right after they left, I had a bout of diarrhea. No headache, vomiting, coughing or cold symptoms. Nothing could stop it until I got a drug called doxycycline mono. It caused us to skip the first two days in Key West from 12/21-28 to 12/24-28. Cam and the three kids came back on 2/15-18/20. Then Joyce got sick with a long week or so dry cough from 2/19 to 28 before medicine helped her shake it. In both our cases it could have been that the symptoms just ran their courses. The more that is revealed by testing for antibodies seems to indicate that this plague was here possibly months before it showed itself. Not to mention the incompetence of Uncle Crazy in dealing with it.

Continuous rain today which we desperately need. Florida lobster tails grilled tonight.

April 25, 2020

DAY 43

Finally got the lobster tail split correctly last night without mangling the meat! Between that and the dark roux, Chef Jimmy had a good week! Joyce's grilled Romaine lettuce was terrific, too. Love talking about the food as cooking it. It is the first hobby of my life. Tonight, we feature a veggie frittata and honey corn bread.

Something is going to break in Ft Myers I have a feeling. They are in a lengthy room reservation cancellation period which cuts into the first week of our family vacation. Seems like a harsh move and it just might be overturned. Surprise of the pandemic…our governor has been sounding cautious and careful of late about re-opening---beaches, restaurants, bars and indoor venues. Something we natives fear…if he re-opens too fast, you Yankees will come flocking back and that could be a disaster.

April 26, 2020

DAY 44

Two good conversations today with the "Commissioner" Dick Langton and Dave Malone in Philadelphia.

It really got my spirits up which were sagging a tad to talk to two dear friends…one 87, the other 60. Quite an age spread. Good convertible ride that seemed to pep up Joyce. Thought we were going to get caught in the rain with the top down and no place to stop. Made it into the garage. Pizza tonight.

April 27, 2020

DAY 45

Lawn guy not here yet. Joyce and I cleaned out the front landscaping, got rid of the old solar lights and the pots. Ken coming to finalize the re-do plans. Melita at 1:00 for an estimate on lanai paint job.

April 28, 2020

DAY 46

Ken here to finalize the front landscaping…should start any day! Melita sent an acceptable estimate and the lanai paint job will start Thursday. Took in my golf cart charger and was surprised to hear it could be fixed! Tried to buy two N95 masks but the place was closed. Will try tomorrow. Our Governor DeSantis has endeared himself to us ancients by referring to Florida as God's Waiting Room. Quite an outcry from the senior set…but he is partially right! #NotAFloridaMoron. Got an upsetting phone call from Cait last night. Very emotional on her part as well as the kids. A cooler head would say that the sequester was taking its toll. Sent the boys back to their dad and Jordan to Dayton. Poor little Julia better keep her mouth shut. Fettucine and sausage tonight.

April 29, 2020

DAY 47

Joyce's favorite tonight…all veggies and some tiny Yukon Golds. Roasted eggplant with parmesan and mozzarella, sliced tomatoes, the same. Carrots, red peppers and onions. Bought those KN95 masks, K standing for Korean. Further fallout from Gurnee. Jeez! You try to gift someone for a tremendous achievement and all hell breaks loose. And you love everyone involved, except one.

April 30, 2020

Day 48 (another month gone by!)

Yet, it is not a wasted month. Studying Spanish on Duolingo and have been amazingly consistent with it, for me!

Yo tengo un maleto. Lo esta aqui.

Also, reading Rutherford's monster historical fiction "Sarum."

I have a couple of gripes and I have been kind of good about not whining. I have asthma which kicked up, after many years dormant last May. Started puffing a Symbicort and it works great, but my lungs are still subject to respiratory problems and Covid-19 stalks me. Also, I cannot travel...finally got the money to do so and the best travel partner in the world and we are stuck here indefinitely. However, to do your lock-up in 80 degrees weather, in a multi-bedroom house, with several hundred books and our beautiful art collection is not bad.

Cherry cobbler tonight and am trying to sneak in some chili dogs, too.

May 1, 2020

DAY 49

"April sighed and stepped aside and along came pretty little May..." Carousel!!!

Payday!! Glad it keeps showing up after almost 19 years! How about continuing with the new name of for sheltering: The ultimate Groundhog Day!

May 2, 2020

DAY 50

A fabulous take-out dinner from a new Creole restaurant in town called H'OURS. Joyce had butter fish and an artichoke salad and bourbon pecan pie. I had the best BBQ ribs and slaw. Wonderful dinner. John Mascari is doing better after his latest infusion. Chatted briefly with my neighbor Shirley Newton on our way to take-out. Amazing how a conversation with a friend can renew your spirits. Tarpon Springs is slowly opening on Monday. Beaches and restaurants first. Holding out hope for a family vacation in Ft Myers in July. Beaches open, reservations taken as of 5/15, but a question about time shares yet to be resolved.

May 3, 2020

DAY 51 (seems just like yesterday)

Anxiously awaiting tomorrow here in God's Waiting Room (Florida) to see how the partial re-opening goes. Some nitwit restaurant owner in Dunedin wants to have a gala re-opening party at his place. Just the hyperbolic words are enough to scare us. Of course, he assured everyone that distance and all guidelines would be followed. There is not a single place where Joyce and I want to go under the current conditions. What is cool is that our favorite brewery, The Liquid Garage, is selling "growlers" curbside. If you are too young, look growlers up!

If the cacophony of Covid-19 noise emitted from dozens of critics has you baffled, I would recommend you read Heather Cox Richardson. Look up her bona fides on Wikipedia and catch her amazing opinion pieces on FB or elsewhere.

However long the duration of this thing is, we plan to stay in weeks after the re-openings are even successful. Maybe until a vaccination arrives. Been everywhere from Canada to Key West to Venezuela and Cuba and much of the Caribbean, Africa, China and all over Mexico, Europe and the UK. Forty-one states here. Have eaten in many great restaurants. Had so many adventures… helicoptered into the Grand Canyon for a champagne picnic, Hot air ballooned from Kenya into Tanzania, para-sailed 1000 feet over the Gulf, dove in several Caribe and Mexican spots, ran three marathons, hiked to the top of El Capitan in Yellowstone, swam with the sharks in Marathon, FL, spent 14 months sequestered in a monastery, 6 ½ years in a religious order, lived for a month each in San Miguel and Florence, been published a few times, a teacher for 37 years and a retiree for nineteen, a union organizer, and married three times, one divorce, one death and one forever! Two kids, one adopted, two others taken in and seven grandchildren.

Ready to chill for however long with my little honey, my wife Joyce Renneke Sweeney.

May 4, 2020

DAY 52

Took another tour today. The beaches, restaurants and motels are opened. No mad dash we noticed. Went to the beaches first. Visited Anclote River Park, a small beach that is more of a boat entry spot. Lots of boats in, but orderly and not overcrowded. Fred Howard Park, our Tarpon Springs island beach, is accessed by a milelong concourse. Again, proper spacing there and parking, which is usually a rarity. Lots of deputies monitoring. Same at our favorite spot, Sunset Beach. Looked so inviting we parked and sat on a bench in the sun for about a half hour. Just looking at the folks sunbathing, walking or reading on the beaches makes one wonder if anything is really going on or worrying anybody.

Went to Publix in the afternoon and talked to my favorite cashier and bagger guy about customers not masking. Both were pissed off, as I have been for days. Main culprits seem to be old ladies! Why? Not a clue!

Suggested to Joyce that maybe we are overdosing again on Covid-19 news and coverage. Get the impression not everyone is. We take all the precautions, but others just seem to glide through these days.

May 5, 2020

DAY 53 (Cinco de Mayo, or the day the ship bearing five tons of Mayonnaise to Mexico sank)

Took Joyce's car in and then went to Sunset Beach. No crowding…good distance. Enjoyed the sun for about 45 minutes. So good to look upon the water again. Melita's guy has the first coat of paint on the lanai and it looks great! Stopped to get some Tequila and Cointreau for margaritas and called Sip85 for tacos…delicious! Back still hurting. I think I strained a muscle pulling the bands. Lotta' heat and ice packs. Great talk with Charley Yanz who never fails to delight. Was happy he is observing quarantine. Cannot afford to lose one of my closest friends. Two episodes of Ozark tonight. Wendy emerging as a major player.

May 6, 2020

DAY 54

Back better but still sore. Corn bread and broccoli and ham quiche…good!
Drank too much so in bed at 8:30. Useless!

May 7, 2020

Day 55

Lanai done. Furniture back in place. It looks fabulous. Love gutsy little Melita
the Rumanian who runs her own business and takes no bs from anyone. I wrote
her check and went to the grocery and forgot to tell Joyce it was on my desk so
Melita did not get paid. I was scared she was mad. But she came by the next day
and got her check plus a tip I ask her to give Oliver. Got a big kick out of this tiny
girl…she took a step back, saluted me and said "Yessir."

Ethnic dinner…a baked potato each. Before the famine in Ireland, a hard-
working Irish laborer ate fourteen to sixteen potatoes a day!

May 8, 2020

DAY 56

The front landscaping is done. Ken and the boys did a fabulous job! Tiny multicolored rocks and minimalist plants make for a stunning look, complete with solar ground lights. Since January we have replaced fans and foyer lights indoors and out, remodeled a guest bathroom, painted and added a splashboard in the kitchen, refinished the lanai floor and cleaned out a mess of vegetation along the southside of the house.

Raw shrimp, delicious mussels, French bread and Mont Ste. Michel Sauvignon Blanc for a tasty respite.

Episode 5 of *The Last Dance* documentary, the Chicago Bulls incredible championship runs! Endlessly intriguing! No need to comment on this great series. I lived every day of it and every nuance, insult delivered, intrigue...everything about the whole organization was noted and known immediately to the city of Chicago! We lived and died by it! Not much more to be said.

May 9, 2020

DAY 57

A rather dead day...almost a letdown since our projects are done. Moped around until dinner but came through with a grand slam! Two perfectly done filets, tiny Yukon potatoes and a great mushroom sauce of 'rooms, pan drippings, red wine, beef broth and a tad of corn starch! Mother's Day came last night!

May 10, 2020

DAY 58 (Mother's Day)

Posted an old almost sepia tone picture of my mom in her early twenties on Facebook. Straight, I said, from an F. Scott Fitzgerald short story. Amazing responses! My mom? Not so much a Daisy, more of a Jordan Baker or a Judy Jones.

Why has the coronavirus, bad as it is here in FL, not reached epic proportions? It was predicted after a huge start in Broward and Dade counties that the state would reach 465,700 hospitalized cases by April 24. We have currently about 4800 cases. There is no strain on our facilities as we carefully re-open in phases. People here stayed in way before a state-wide mandate required it.

Joke all you want about senior citizens here. They make up 23% of our 22,000,000 population and they are not dumb people. They have managed to stay alive through a multitude of personal and societal problems. They had careers good enough to afford coming to this comfortable environment with money and good health. They did not get to this point by making stupid choices and they are not going to begin now. This not a redneck, cracker group. The six largest counties, Dade, Broward, Pinellas, Duval and Palm Beach and Hillsborough comprise the biggest population group in the state and went for Obama twice. Hard as it is to say, I applaud Gov. DeSantis. He has operated slowly, maybe too slowly, but with measured restraint. He has recovered from the Spring Break fiasco at Clearwater Beach and will only continue to be successful if we continue masking and distancing. Two other things distinguish our good fortune from other locales…due to our lack of urban density we have little public transportation. There are no crowded buses or subways or trains.

#notafloridamoron

May 11, 2020

DAY 59

The ground level flat solar lights in the new front lawn configuration are not on after two days of absorbing sunlight. Finally, Joyce went out and pulled one up in a dark area, pushed the button and VOILA! Seems Ken planted them all but forgot to push the activating button. Now those bad boys light up the whole area in the coolest fashion!

If I figure correctly the 80 deaths in Pinellas County consist of 42 nursing home persons ranging from 77 to 94 years of age. Stay home, but out of A NURSING HOME!

Dinner tonight: French Toast and sausage!

May 12, 2020

DAY 60

A sneeze is worse than a cough, projection-wise. A sneeze blasts off from your nose and mouth with a velocity of 200 miles per hour.

Great news: NFL should be on 9/10/2020. Just so they are on TV…Bucs and Brady!

Cool exchange with my cousin Tom's daughter Kathy Vincent last night about the inability of Ohio to get unemployment insurance up and running. What a sweet kid!

May 13, 2020

DAY 61

My nephew Matt Hite, 48, was found dead yesterday, I think. I know he died but not sure if the day he was found is the day he died. Sounds like the beginning lines of *The Stranger*. He was found dead on the 12th, but people were trying to reach him over last few days before Mother's Day and could not. He was grossly overweight, maybe 300 plus lbs. It could have been heart failure, apnea or even covid-19 which moved from asymptomatic and joined in with other issues. He had little if any health insurance and probably ignored his health. As a cook, he had been out of work for probably two months or more. And like Kathy Vincent said above, he too probably did not get any Ohio unemployment. RIP, old buddy!

May 14, 2020

DAY 62

Here is my updated list...John Martin, Pete Sakas, Bill Richardson, Dave Schusteff, Liz Salicete, Matt Hite and Larry Poltrock. RIP...No more new names!

May 15, 2020

DAY 63

Reflecting extremely hard on the plight of my sister and her husband. To lose a child, no matter the age, is devastating, as I can only imagine. Especially, when he appears to have died alone in no one knows what kind of circumstances. That is haunting. I hate to say this, but the happiness must have gone out of their lives. This situation and the grief will never leave. And at 80 and 81, not many years are left to come to grips with it. When Jerri Rae's death occurred, I almost felt relief at her freedom from 24 years of cancer. But it took a while, after the cremation, two memorial services and various settlements, for her death to fully grab my psyche. And the pain came, always unannounced, and almost broke me. I drank in excess one day after trying to exhaust myself with work and golf in 100 degrees temp just to get some sleep. I fell and cracked open my head, jostling grey matter. Finally got a friend to call the EMTs who got me to the hospital and then to another one who had a neurosurgeon on duty. I survived despite having an alcohol content three times the sober level. This was how I coped until I gradually pulled myself out of this extreme and dangerous behavior. Now they must face this unnatural occurrence, a child dying before a parent. My loss was normal, not tragic. Theirs' is dealing with the life of their beloved son extinguished, probably unfulfilled and in circumstances unknown. Sent a card of condolences with a check today.

May 16, 2020

DAY 64

In this time of death and isolation I look anywhere for surcease of sorrow. From *New Iberia Blues* by James Lee Burke:

"I knew that I no longer had to reclaim the past, that the past was still with me, inextricably part of my soul and who I was; I could step through a hole in the dimension and be with my father and mother again, and I didn't have to drink or mourn the dead or live on a cross for my misdeeds; I was set free and the past and the future and the present were at the ends of my fingertips, filled with promise and goodness, and I didn't have to submit to time or fate or even mortality…and I realized finally that the invitation to it comes with the sunrise and a clear eye and a good heart and the knowledge that we're already inside eternity and need not fear any longer."

Only through Joyce, who is my portal to the future!

May 17, 2020

No more writing about a certain topic.

The only way to counter the current assault upon our constitution, our rules of governing and our way of life is to fight as passionately for democracy as Trump's cultists fight for fascism. However, we probably will not!

Just picking out one social upheaval that altered our way of life, I choose WWII. From it came the rebuilding of Europe, and the biggest change in education...the GI Bill... that sent thousands of young men to college who never would have thought to go there. It unleashed the most dynamic and productive era in manufacturing, made home ownership possible, created the suburbs and guaranteed the growth of the family unit plus much more, including the Cold War.

This pandemic might not equal WWII in duration, but it must bring about social, educational, environmental and economic changes in much that needs changing, especially in the roles of women in the workforce and politics.

May 18, 2020

Not a lot…got gas, went to the bank, grocery store, checked out the reopened health club and returned books to the library. Reticent about breaking out of the Q, both of us. Only time will tell how this goes, but for sure where we live in Pinellas County, north end, the spread is relatively mild. The secretary of our Homeowners Association does not know of a sickness within Crescent Oaks. Made tuna salad…and tuna melts for dinner, talked to Cami twice today and had a marathon listening festival with the beloved Aunt Mary, Jerri Rae's sister. Uncle Crazy IQ45 announced he is taking hydroxychloroquine. Maybe, Maybe not. If a side effect is brain damage, how will we know?

May 19, 2020

Day 67

President Tweety...I like that! Kudos to Joe Biden! Chinese tonight! First orange beef and spring rolls and veggie fried rice in months. Considering going to the Zone, our health club, once a week. Need a bigger workout. Looks safe. No decision yet. Stats says Florida is doing well. Lags way behind Texas and California in cases and deaths and we are the third largest behind those two. Feel somewhat secure in Pinellas County, but statewide there is always the question of testing. If you have an increase in cases, they are not necessarily new, just undiscovered ones hidden by not testing. So, I take this "good" news with the usual grain of Morton's. One can easily see why President Goofy is against testing---no "new" cases as if testing created the virus in someone!

Give re-opening results another couple of weeks, especially in Wisconsin!

May 20, 2020

When you think about an unconscionable act remember this: Never say you had no plan in mind when you set out innocently and end up doing or saying something possibly objectionable or worse. Your unconscious mind always knows what you are doing or planning or about to do, but it never says anything. It lets your conscious mind do the dirty work of finding the appropriate situation and rationale that justifies you and gives you permission to say some words or do some deeds that are unconscionable. Distrust the man who says he is without a plan! He is just unaware that he has one!

May 21, 2020

We watched *Cocoon* last night. Previously seen 36 years ago, but worth watching again. The recently passed Brian Dennehy, playing an alien posing as a human being, brought grace, dignity and strength to a role that a lesser actor would have made comedic. There was a real question posited here...not necessarily a moral one, but one more on a philosophical note. Apart from the fun of watching geezers frolic like kids in the pod filled pool, the movie asks: is the question of living life in its natural progression—birth, youth, middle age, old age, death preferable to living forever? Dean Swift answered that in Gulliver's Travels quite effectively centuries ago. Yes, the natural progression is preferable. But this film has it both ways. The choice to go to a distant planet for eternal life is posited. Just after losing his wife, surprisingly Harvey, the retirement group's contrarian, does not go simply because he "belongs here." Wilfred Brimley and Maureen Stapleton happily leave their only daughter and only grandson for the promise of living forever! We failed to remember the ending and guessed incorrectly that they would never leave. Wrong! Think the question through and take your pick... Funny how old people are not so funny this time around.

One of the great paradoxes of existence is that one's life only has value in relation to one's awareness and acknowledgement of the finality of death!

May 22, 2020

DAY 70

Message to any of my relatives concerning my nephew's death: "I think there is no point to me even asking about it. I will never hear. But I did love the kid and hate to think of him dying alone."

Uncle Crazy's meandering diction and syntax:

"I tested very positively in another sense so—this morning. Yeah. I tested positively toward negative, right. So, I tested perfectly this morning. Meaning I tested negative. But that is a way of saying it. Positively toward the negative." Got that, everyone?

May 23, 2020

DAY 71

My donation to hospitality workers in the name of my recently dead nephew was cashed yesterday. And, presumably, will be paid to the appropriate group by my sister. At least it showed up in the mail within my card…spared me from asking if it got there and putting a stop on it if it had not. The whole intent was to avoid any conversation. Time to move on…

May 24, 2020

Day 72

Happy Birthday to the best wife ever! Little Joyce is smart, tough and resilient! She has lived about three lifetimes, walked away from some marital mishaps, raised two extremely competent daughters on her own, got a college degree, bought her own house, travelled extensively and made great salaries and totally captivated me. I cannot imagine life without her now. I just say I am the title of Kingsley Amis' best novel *Lucky Jim!*

And she treats me like Joseph Conrad's *Lord Jim.* This is our fourth birthday together and I hope there are many, many more!

Rubbed down with a million spices and marinated for six hours the biggest fucking sirloin for her birthday dinner…complete with green beans and French fries. Carrot cake to follow!

May 25, 2020

DAY 73

"We call love what binds us to certain creatures only by reference to a collective way of seeing for which books, songs, poems and legends are responsible. But of love I know only that mixture of desire, affection and intelligence that binds me to this or that creature. That compound is not the same for another person... There is no noble love but that which recognizes itself to be both short-lived and exceptional." (Camus, *The Myth of Sisyphus*) This quote goes a long way in explaining one's desires and activities. These constant deaths and rebirths apparently flower in many men. But guilt makes them hard to renew while, at the same time, offering them their piquant nature that is so attractive.

May 26, 2020

DAY 74

A thank you note from my sister arrived acknowledging my donation. "I know you had a bond with Matt. Two BSers." Whatever!!!! "Whatever" is as dismissive as I can be in response to the nature of her characterization of me and her son. Me...does not matter, but him...Nothing will bring that BSer back.

May 27, 2020

DAY 75

Dropped Duolingo. Getting repetitive and boring plus never going to really learn it, anyway. George Floyd is dead. The cop taking a knee, Derek Chavun, has been cited 12 times for various complaints, but no disciplinary action taken. A nineteen years veteran of the Minneapolis PD. Riots, looting and fires probably will continue. Charges better follow or flames will increase, I predict.

A cruise ship leaving Argentina checked everyone coming aboard and rejected all who had been in covid-19 hot spots. Eight aboard still got sick and were dropped off. The remaining folks were tested and, of the total, 81% were positive, but asymptomatic. Extrapolate that to the general population and the importance of testing reaches huge proportions. Where is the testing???? Possible 80% of the population is feeling fine while spreading the virus! WEAR THE FUCKING MASK!!!!!

May 28, 2020

DAY 76

"There are words I have never really understood such as sin. For if there is a sin against life, it consists perhaps not so much in despairing of life as in hoping for another life and in eluding the implacable grandeur of this life...From Pandora's Box, where all the ills of humanity swarmed, the Greeks drew out hope after all the others, as the most dreadful of all. I know no more stirring symbol; for, contrary to the general belief, hope equals resignation (or as others have said "philosophical suicide") And to live is not to resign oneself." (Camus, *The Myth of Sisyphus*.)

First outsider reading by Joyce. Wonder what the verdict will be? Picnic tonight! She likes it!

Late night entry: My wife's hometown is in flames and not only Minneapolis but St. Paul, also. A three-headed monster: Trump, Covid-19, and continuing economic disruption/ racism is consuming our country!

May 29, 2020

DAY 77 (14 the hard way!)

We are mesmerized by the actions in Minneapolis. Joyce was born and raised in Deephaven, a near suburb, attended U of M, and considers herself a native. She was aware of the locations of fires and protests last night. Minneapolis has always struck me as a clean, wholesome place seemingly free of normal urban problems and strife. I always associated the Twin Cities with strong minded labor activists and great political coalitions, as per Eric Sevareid's memoir *Not So Wild A Dream.* True enough then but naïve thinking on my part now. The world has turned upside down and my romantic notions of robust equality and democratic principles are out the window. Will charges be filed today? I think not but wait to be corrected.

And corrected I am! Officer Derek Chauvin, the neck kneeler, has been arrested and charged with third degree murder and manslaughter as a legal back up position. Not sure where the protest goes tonight, but the Floyd family and the people on the street are not happy. They want first degree murder and the other three charged. But taking a winning position is always the most important thing. My beloved Louisville looking shaky tonight over the mistaken killing of an EMH worker in March that remains unresolved as I write. Signing off for tonight.

Ozark ended today for us. Meatballs and spaghetti tonight!

May 30, 2020

DAY 78

This is a day we all should be celebrating, but the main event is lost in the swirling miasma of a nascent revolution in our country.

SpaceX, a private corporation, launches the amazingly engineered Falcon 9 rocket into orbit with two NASA astronauts aboard. The first such firing in nine years and the first collaboration between private enterprise and the US government ever! Docking at a space station and returning to planet Earth in four months is its' goal. Godspeed!

Now to the revolution. I would never say this in a conversation except with my wife nor would I publicly write it on FB, but I hope the protests continue despite the injuries, possible deaths and property damage. No revolution has ever been nonviolent and this one has been long coming. We should see it to some dramatically changing ending and not have to do it over yearly.

Trump, Covid-19, racial injustice and revolution...what a brew! Our president and Attorney General lie daily. Do not believe them! There is only the alt-right (Proud Boys, White Supremacists, foreign influences) that are intervening and bringing about violence and destruction. This has been proven by Minneapolis police statistics gathered from people hauled in.

I think Minneapolis will regret the heavy-handed police action of last night. Was it necessary to unload on an obviously peaceful group? The pristine reputation of "Minnesota Nice" may be in jeopardy. Jah, you bet!

If armed thugs are looting, and a loot/shoot order is in effect to protect state and local governments, what should be done to armed thugs who protest and threaten duly elected officials over their legitimate stay-in rules? Answer that, Trump/Barr!!!

June 1, 2020

DAY 79

First day of hurricane season for us in Florida and not ending until November 30…much on our proverbial plates.

What the immediate solution up north might be and how it might be accomplished all rests in Minneapolis and what its' citizens decide. The police there, like police everywhere, are intensely tribal. In most cases, this is a good occupational thing. You absolutely must trust your partner and your squad members and the officers who supervise you. Yet this can calcify into a blind loyalty over time, a loyalty that can replace honest criticism and assessment and lead to the acceptance of ethical shoddiness and outright wrongdoing. Challenging this code can lead to shunning and potential danger on the job.

As a former teacher union officer, I know something about tribalism. God help the teacher who crossed our picket line. He/she would be ignored, looked down upon, and in general, isolated by one's colleagues…as they probably still say in tough East St. Louis; "if a scab calls for help dealing with a student threatening assault, you ignore him." Still, teachers, unlike cops, generally are not in danger for their lives, but the analogy has some validity.

Cops killing black men is not a problem that can be surgically and delicately dealt with. It requires a blunt instrument. There is not going to be mass conversions to goodness and gentleness among police forces. The only thing that will work is to frighten a cop with loss of job, pension, prison time and a felony tag for the rest of his life if he engages in the kind of activity that police forces have engaged in in most cities. George Floyd is now a national symbol for protesters in major cities and is a stand-in for their local police brutality griev-ance. Minneapolis must arrest the other policemen and charge them as accesso-ries as they charged the kneeler with third degree murder. A message must be sent! The ball is in your court, Minneapolis.

We visited a bookstore in Dunedin, purchased some books and ate lunch outdoors at The Living Room restaurant. Two firsts!

June 2, 2020

DAY 80

Going with a bit of silence today so I can enjoy my two new books: Hilary Mantel's final in the Cromwell trilogy *The Mirror and The Lamp* and Scott Turow's latest courtroom novel featuring Sandy Stern.

See what happens tonight! Meatloaf, little potatoes and peas.

June 3, 2020

DAY 81

Little brother, Long Tom's birthday! He is 73!

Charges are finalized against all four Minneapolis cops…Up to you, Hennepin County!

June 4, 2020

DAY 82

I hope some of the destructive steam will go out of the protests, nationwide. Not wanting them to end, though. The charges against the cops, placed and/or upgraded, should satisfy most, but the pressure must be kept on, especially in DC so that bastard in the WH always remembers how much he is hated. I especially fear new Covid-19 outbreaks due to the lack of distancing by the multi-city crowds. There is only one goal to be achieved as far as I am concerned. And that is to convict these cops and send the message to all of them to stop this murderous tendency or they will be arrested, convicted and imprisoned.

The Republican Senate continues to model its cowardice when questioned about Trump's activities. Only Romney spoke out as did Lisa Murkowski who will eventually change her mind and recant her position. The rest were either late for lunch or never read newspapers or watch television!

I have mastered the cutting and grilling of the Florida Spiny Lobster and its close relative, the Bahamian Lobster.

June 5, 2020

DAY 83

Commissioner Goodell admits "we were wrong," in handling the issue of player protests. And he apologized for not listening to NFL players and encouraging all to speak out and protest peacefully. Colin Kaepernick was right in 2016 and is now acknowledge as right by the NFL Office, but still not hired. Poor Drew Brees cannot get out of his own way while trying to respect the flag, the presidency, and America. OK. Why then does he apologize? Because he is tone deaf as to what is going on as I write. But his apology rings hollow on many black NFL ears. Then his buddy Trump bitches him out for apologizing, so he tells Bunker Don he is wrong and, inadvertently, gets that right! Who can clarify things for this misguided jock?

What will be interesting is the forms of protest held by teams if the season ever gets started. The Detroit Lions have already joined a peaceful protest crowd as well as the Denver Broncos and others. If you vowed never to watch the NFL again after Kap took a knee, you might as well throw your Samsung out the window or learn to love a good rugby match. Team protests will be rehearsed like end zone choreographies. Team members will fight to be included. Half-time shows will be so last season as protest clips vie for ESPN's bests of the week slots! No more knee capping Kap. No contract for him, but he is finally getting his due!

June 6, 2020

DAY 84 (D-DAY)

Uncle Bob and Uncle Dave served and survived! Rained all day and Hurricane Cristobal to land around Slidell, LA tomorrow! Will get to Normandy one of these days. Still remembering the US Military Cemetery between Florence and Siena in the Tuscan region of Italy, maintained by the US Department of Defense and secured by Italian forces. Curious...they were our enemy. Hallowed ground.

I wrote this poem in 1994 to commemorate a group of former WWII paratroopers, most in their seventies, who celebrated the 50th anniversary of D-Day by re-enacting their dives into Normandy velcroed to real paratroopers!

The Day Before D-Day---1994

Old men dot a French sky./Like Icarus/Restored to fly./A daring, silken, wafting, mythic/Way to die,/If they might die./Yet they must fly./To bring a pledge full circle,/To fulfill a trust/To young men/Who dotted a French sky./Two score and a half ago:/Omaha, Juno, Ste-Mere-Eglise, Ste. Lo.

June 7, 2020

I brought up Olympic diver Bruce Kimball's name to Joyce today as a redemptive contrast to Lance Armstrong. She had never heard of him. His catastrophic incident occurred in Brandon, FL, a suburb of Tampa where she worked for years. We had watched ESPN's 30 on 30 on Armstrong yesterday and could only conclude that he is a lying, self-centered jerk. He has a curious self-deprecating way…he refers to himself as a "fucking asshole. There…I admitted it! Now I can do or say anything I want." No remorse, no regret, at least none to which he admitted. Guys ratted him out. They are to blame. Lance involved the whole team in illegal drugging so they would protect him while protecting themselves. Diabolically clever insurance ploy. I think the guy has so many scenarios in his head that he is never sure which one to bring out and live by, even if temporarily. But he is a cheater who exists with this lie every day.

However, Lance never killed anybody…he broke hearts, wrecked careers and probably got money illegally. Diver Bruce Kimball did kill two people and seriously maimed two others driving drunkenly into a crowd. But his is a story of punishment served, forgiveness sought and maybe some degree of redemption achieved. For another time or Google the entire story.

June 8, 2020

DAY 86

Gutters and roof being cleaned today…gutters are impacted with leaves from the seven trees on our quarter acre property. Have spent a ton of money since January on the house. New interior hall and foyer lights and fans, guest bathroom with paint job, tub removal, new shower stall and fixtures, and tiled floor. Partial kitchen paint job and splash board, new front landscaping and major sod replacement, and lanai floor repainted and now this gutter job. Never ending maintenance!

Just got a red beans and rice recipe that looks terrific!

June 9, 2020

DAY 87

A magnificent sunrise at 6:40 am! Pale blue sky streaked with pink and gold cloud slivers. The soft beauty of a Florida early morning is incomparable. The sky is dotted with birds going to work. My phone camera tried but could not capture the subtlety of it all, nor can my words, ever.

Exactly six months from today I will be 80 years old…now only zeros and fives count. This will be a big one.

Here is a piece by Leslie Dwight, a gifted young lady, that is all over FB and Instagram. It fits perfectly with the emerging and ongoing themes of my journal! Thank you, Miss!

"What if 2020 isn't cancelled?

What if 2020 is the year we have been waiting for?

A year so uncomfortable, so painful, so scary, so raw---

That it finally forces us to grow.

A year that screams so loud, finally awaken us

From our ignorant slumber.

A year we finally accept the need for change.

Declare change. Work for change. Become the change.

A year we finally band together, instead of

Pushing each other further apart.

2020 is not cancelled, but rather

The most important year of them all." (Leslie Dwight, 2020)

She is exactly right…2020 is just warming up! The year of the perfect witches' brew: Trump, Covid-19 and the murder of George Floyd which is raising a multitude of ignored social, financial and racial issues. It will rank with 1968, maybe even exceed it!

I am going to continue this journal daily until my birthday, 12/09/2020. I am going to publish it, print one hundred copies and send them to select recipients. Title to be determined.

June 10, 2020

DAY 88 (fat #'s day!)

I wish progressive democrats would shut up about Joe Biden. For the most part, they are going to vote for him as an alternative to Trump. But one would think they were being asked to swallow broken glass! Biden is "demented, good for about another year of life, Hillary-lite and a member of the dreaded DNC cabal (Clintons, Obama, Wassermann-Schultz et. al.)" Their guy, Bernie, sank like a stone in the primaries never to be heard from again. He only spoke long enough to tell his people to vote for Biden so another loss to Trump would not be attributed to him. It sometimes seems that progressives could care less if Trump wins. I like Joe. He reminds me of myself when I labored in Labor's fields. I was a glad-handing, back slapping, smiling Irishman, quick with a quip and Uncle Jim assurances. I bet my organizer daughter listens to my stories and advice with large dose of patience. Joe and I are from a different era. I like his wife. She is accomplished, attractive and feisty like mine. Both would leap to our defense if needed. These needling attacks and the constant reminders of his flaws may just encourage those more to the left to abandon him and stick to their mission of destroying the DNC rather than driving the beast out of office!

June 11, 2020

DAY 89

Housekeeping...I took Joyce to the dentist to have a tooth pulled this morning, to be replaced in a couple of months. Sore mouth and cheek. I got her some broccoli and cheese soup from Panera's for dinner tonight. Talked to Cait last night. She, Dave and Jordan will get tested before coming down on 6/25. It is amazing how one's thinking changes, usually for the better, in times like these. I had called Bob Johnson in North Port and suggested that Joyce and I meet him and Hector for lunch in Venice on our way to Ft. Myers Beach. It occurred to me that I should tell Bob that we had been with family from Chicago two days previous. He must have the option to accept or reject our lunch offer. I called Cait. Joyce and I decided to get tested as did Cam and her friend Ann before they came down. There are seven kids involved ranging from 3 to 14. Testing is probably not necessary for all the kids and none of us adults have symptoms, but still...test everyone in sight!

We will be at Ft Myers Beach from 6/27 until 7/11, one week with each daughter and family. I miss them very much.

Got a great thank you message from Clarence P. Jones for our card and gift to the soon to be married couple. They will still get married on the 6/22, but without the guests and reception due to the Covid-19. Also got a thank you note from the service industry fund for unemployed workers in Columbus for our donation in Matt's name. They said they knew him and that he had a wonderful smile.

June 12, 2020

DAY 90

I wish I were young again and the current protest situation could use my response. But it is not my game. My biggest challenge is staying alive for Joyce and the kids. The best I can do is be a good person, as good as I can be, and model some kindness. Stop sarcastically putting down people on FB. Stop showing off my "assumed" intelligence. It always backfires. Keep treating our work folks with praise and tips. Let us just survive the next five months and put Trump behind us. This is a time for young people to rise up like we did in 1968, our last seminal year, and rework this country into something remarkable again. And that can only be achieved by facing, once and for all, our everlasting original sins... slavery and racism!!!

June 13, 2020

Day 91

President Trump referred to the Secret Service as the 'SS' recently. He also described in detail the police and National Guard response to protestors in Lafayette Park as a "beautiful scene." "They cut right down the middle and went through them like a knife through butter. It was beautiful, to me." He (and Barr) authorized an attack upon America citizens exercising their First Amendment right to peaceably protest. Similar situations arose during the civil rights demonstrations. I was there and saw them. But those were locally done by known racists and racist groups, Never has an American president ordered such an attack, in his presence, so he could have a photo op in front of a church holding a bible, which he has never read and in front of a church he has never attended.

When I think about him, read about him and write about him, I CAN'T BREATHE!!!

June 14, 2020

DAY 92 (Another cop on black murder in Atlanta)

This is another piece attempting to deal with a question I raised before. I thought the progressive wing of the democrat party had come to grips with Joe Biden and their perceived notions of his old age, forgetfulness and encroaching dementia. The kindest thing they could say was they hoped he picked a progressive vice president because he would never live through a full term. But they did seem resolved to vote for him just to get rid of Trump. Sounded logical to me, but what do I know? Lately, particularly from Chicago progressives and a few FB thinkers, I hear those old refrains again. A Biden presidency is the same as a Republican one…no difference. Even though nothing of social value strictly for average people has ever come from a republican administration since Lincoln died. I can't seem to find the people who think and write to agree that Biden is 100% better than Trump under any circumstances or who can't see that Bernie, the president without portfolio, can have his way with Joe, progressively speaking, so I will frame my solution a different way.

(Satire alert…This is for young progressives who hate Biden) The time to make the break is now while we are in the mood to do away with stuff! We should withhold our Biden votes, especially in contentious electoral college areas, and give Trump a free path! That way the evil and bloated DNC can be obliterated along with the entire party structure. We can once and for all do away with the Clintons/Obama/Biden/Wasserman-Schulz/Perez cabal and eradicate the stains they left behind. A new party must arise…A Peoples' Progressive Socialist Party! However, be wary of new titles and slogans, like "Defund the Police" (you see how that turned out). No more delegate apportioning, super delegates, platform pandering, big donors (a thousand bucks limit), strong arm unions or Hollywood and coastal elites. Four more years of Trump is a small price to pay for this golden opportunity to eliminate the recent rotten past of the old democrat party and determine and define eternally progressive principles and set them forth clearly and cogently. A 2024 election could not be easier if this is done right! It is all for the new order if that is what my former democrat colleagues want!

Another black man found hanging in a tree in Palmdale, California! Jesus wept!

June 15, 2020

DAY 93

Testing Day...Druid at Myrtle in Clearwater. Lots of procedures...Never leave the car, get in car line, information fill-outs, car line on opposite side of test administration, circle the parking lot onto Druid for a quick left onto Myrtle to enter stage two and await a call from your medical insurer giving you the go-ahead, then to the big tent for a two nostril swabbing and some heartfelt goodbyes. About one hour and a half.

Next stop, Parker Manor on Clearwater Beach, to express our condolences to Dawn and Todt on the loss of husband and father and my old Chicago friend Bud Marks who died of cancer rather quickly on Thursday. Bud and I go way back, but I have known Dawn even longer. She and Jerri Rae taught together for years and I met them while helping organize their union forty five years ago. So much to remember...years of Sunday morning golf with Bud and Bill, our houses at Lake Cora in MI, our Korean adoptions of Caitlen and Molly, and more. And, of course, Bud being almost five years younger provided a stark reminder of my own mortality!

June 16, 2020

DAY 94

Bloomsday in Dublin! A marvelous meal of the simplest ingredients…chicken breasts marinated in Balsamic, olive oil, garlic chips, thyme, and rosemary. Spinach with garlic and, of all things, a side of Mac/cheese from Publix! A chilled Ste Michelle chardonnay topped it off. Joyce had an epiphany (maybe in honor of her namesake James Joyce and Bloomsday!) Sorrow manifested itself to her this evening in an emotional reaction to how viscerally she has been moved by the cries of the families of dead black men, dead at the hands of the police. Like most people living complicated lives, she had been only mildly aware of all the tribulations blacks have felt forever. But, unlike most, her empathy with them now is profound and moving, no matter when it arrived. There is not a hypocritical bone in her body and when she feels something it is from her heart and soul.

June 17, 2020

DAY 94

There is a bird nest, laboriously created, within the confines of a large flowerpot on our porch. The lady in charge is a tiny North Carolina wren with a needle beak and a sassy tail that points straight up! She has black and gold markings which flash away from each eye. Her eggs, hatched or not, are buried in a cave of leaves and building materials she has brought home. When she tends to her flock only her cute little tail sticks out! I constantly remind the lawn guys not to use their loud leaf blower near them. Babies on board! Some bad dude stalked the nest! Caught a glimpse of him this morning, but he must have seen us rush to the window and he took off. Ever vigilant, Sweeney! She is your responsibility now!

June 18, 2020

DAY 95

My FB friend Rick Serley referenced the Saturday Tulsa Trump Rally this morning: Come for the racism; Stay for the plague! Fucking beautiful!

June 19, 2020

DAY 96

Tomorrow's Tulsa Rally threatens to further the pandemic in a city that is seeing a rise in cases and deaths. However, the results of this gathering can be difficult to assess without careful tracing and the passage of time. So far, large gatherings like the pool party in Lake of the Ozarks and the protests nationwide have not borne out the dire predictions. From where is the rapid positive case increases in Florida, Arizona and Texas coming? Apart from the usual suspects, prisons and jails, nursing homes and church gatherings, plus possibly increased testing, it seems to be from millennials ages 25 to 34 who cluster in venues, bars and street gatherings completely ignoring social distancing. How is this related to contagion? If you are close to others in a confined area you are subject to the aerosol effect of one talking, coughing, breathing and laughing and not wearing a mask places you in danger. The masks and the distancing go hand in hand since the only germ provider is one's mouth. The germ has a limited life expectancy in the air when no one is close and is almost nonexistent on surfaces. It is all about proximity to others.

As a safety aside, contagious disease experts now say the beach, apart from clustering with strangers, is probably one of the safest places to recreate because of the continuous breezes. Like soap and water, the wind is the greatest germ diluter.

June 20, 2020

Day 96

Noted that six Trump advance folks have tested positive in Tulsa preparing for the rally. They will be contact traced. Later, I will report on any untoward action outside, during and after. But I refuse to comment on the drivel within. Probably will though since I cannot resist!

OK, drivel update:

"I'm handsomer than them (who?), have better hair, hotels, apartments, golf courses, and homes. Slow down testing for virus, it only produces more cases. Love all blacks, hate Joe. Great ramp walker and water drinker." Ten minutes mocking a disabled walker doing his ramp thing and almost correctly drinking from a water glass. Nothing of substance; tired narrative, underwhelming crowd---great preview of coming rallies and campaign appearances. Some shouting but no violence, MAGA guys seem drained, not willing to engage. No wonder there was a small crowd: Eric Trump twittered: "See you in TULAS, Oklahoma!" God help us all! (Turns out fire dept. calls it 6200 in BOK Center… scads of volunteers, extras, hired ethnics and paid actors. Around 5100 actual MAGAs!) Total bust for Trump. Walk of Shame from his helicopter. Clutching his MAGA hat like a party favor, disheveled, tie askance, exhausted. TIME TO RESIGN?

June 21, 2020

DAY 97

Father's Day...Been one for forty years. Had no idea what I had signed onto and am still learning about it. Big job, but lots of perks, seven big ones for me. Thinking about my dad. A bit distant with words and gestures, but a steady presence who seemed to understand that security and reliability and predictability were probably the best things for a kid to grow up confidently and to feel loved. Would be great to compare notes with him. Thank you, Joyce, for making this a wonderful day!

June 22, 2020

DAY 98

Got my test results right at the last minute today, the seventh day. For the last six days I have been the Covid-19 version of Schrodinger's Cat, the 1935 thought experiment of Erwin Schrodinger. Which stated, if you placed a cat in a box with something that could kill it if certain things happened, you would not know if it was dead or alive until you opened the box. Equivalent to measuring something in quantum physics. It is not fifty-fifty, dead or alive, with the cat. Theoretically, he is both dead and alive until viewed.

I went six days after being tested with no result given me. Therefore, it was not a 50%/50% that I was positive or negative. I was both positive and negative until the results were studied and announced. Negative!!! The cat made it, too. Not a live cat, an imaginary cat in a thought, not real, experiment! My situation is very real!

June 23, 2020

DAY 99

Today, one of Nature's miracles occurred. We had noticed and then carefully watched as a little wren built a nest in a flowerpot of thick moss and ferns on our verandah. Never got close to see what was in there. Once she shot out and scared Joyce. Last week I stopped the yard guy from leaf blowing on the porch so not to disturb them. I stood guard for stalkers. This morning Joyce was in Tampa and I was reading when I heard a scratching noise on the front window screen. There was a tiny North Carolina wren hanging from the screen, mouth agape. Before I could welcome this Tarheel to Tarpon Springs, two more showed up! Mom with her proud trifecta. Joyce got home to enjoy their beginning efforts to fly. I took a ton of pictures and we learned they could only make it about three to five feet up by fluttering their wings. They struggled all afternoon with a lot of rest stops. Then Mom and one baby flew to the roof overhang, sat a moment then flew away. We kept watch. Looked away for a moment and the other two took flight. Never saw them leave. No apparent homing instinct. We are empty nesters again.

June 24, 2020

DAY 100

To what music do lovers respond? Depends on the lovers ages and experiences. We have pretty much decided on the following favorites after nearly four years together:

1. "Losing My Mind," by Stephen Sondheim, sung by Liza Minnelli in a video produced by the Pet Shop Boys.

2. "Harvest Moon," by Neil Young, sung by Neil Young, accompanied by Crazy Horse.

3. "Money for Nothing," by Mark Knopfler, sung by Mark Knopfler and Dire Straits.

4. "Runaway," by Jim Corr, sung by Andrea Corr and The Corrs.

5. "But Beautiful," by Jimmy Van Heusen, sung by Bob Dylan.

June 25, 2020

DAY 101

Cait's family is here: Dave, James, Jordan, John, Julia and Owen. So good to see them...all tested negative, hearing loud voices, eating and drinking and swimming and laughing! Life is good! Took James for a haircut. His head was a cross between a bush and a lampshade. Brett spent an hour or more on him and James is happy, as is his mom. Then...SURPRISE...I took him to an abandoned parking area on US19 and let him drive. Did OK. Building my legacy of memories with my namesake!

Off to Ft Myers Beach tomorrow. Distance and masks and avoidance!!!!! Going to be fine.

"Is there life after death?" "Yes, but not for you!" Harsh? Nope! The sooner one comes to this realization in their life the greater value their life will have. This is it...the tour is on, not to be repeated. Anyone can seize the day, try to squeeze the day. Enough said.

June 26, 2020

DAY 102

This just in! Largest single Florida covid-19 day thus far...nearly 9000 new cases. Twenty-one counties report the largest group testing positive (median age) is under 40! As of 11:00am today: ALL BARS ARE CLOSED. Youthful (25 to 34) disregard for all state and CDC rules brought this about. Restaurants, operating at prescribed capacities, can still serve alcohol at tables. Well played, Governor DeSantis! You are reviled and you fudged the Covid-19 #s, but you did the right thing closing the alcohol bar sales.

June 27, 2020

DAY 103

Off for a hopefully non-precarious vacation to Ft. Myers Beach with Cait's gang first and then Cam's family, the second week. Lahaina, here we come! But first a call from Bob Johnson cancelling lunch in North Port. Sarasota County's surge has made them want to stay home. Good for them for speaking up. Will keep in touch. Long drive. It seems my legs take longer to "get under me" after every drive. Unloaded the car at Lahaina with Joyce, got organized inside and made it to the water. Life-giving salt water! Al-fresco dining tonight reminiscent of Florence—grapes, nuts, sausage slices, crackers, cheese and crudites. I guess we will never get over trying to recreate that magical month in Florence. Everyone here safely!

June 28, 2020

DAY 104

With part of our family at Ft. Myers Beach, FL.

Its' a fact documented by so many authors, Melville, for example, that people rush to the edge of the land to be near the sea. "When there is a cold November in my soul…I know I must take to the sea again." Like people, rivers, streams, creeks, piddling channels rush to meet big waters. Norman Maclean wrote "even in my dreams, a river runs through them." The Paw Paw River runs into, through and out of Maple Lake in Paw Paw, MI. and into the St. Joseph River and on to Lake Michigan. They drained it once and I saw perfect channel boundaries etched into the bottom of the lake. The Mississippi starts by Bemidji, MN and grows into the turgid Big Muddy while the Ohio River rushes to meet it at Cairo, IL to form an almost moving lake delta to New Orleans., I was astounded by the width of the St. John's River south of Jacksonville, FL. And I once rafted the New River rapids in West Virginia, the only river that runs south to north in the USA. I boat toured the St. Lawrence Seaway. I have seen the Thames, the Seine, the Yangtze, the Chicago River, the American River, the Illinois River, the Colorado and endless ocean viewings from many countries. Lakes, rivers and streams lures us. They haunt us by reminding us we are never far from our origins. Its' a major part of our physical makeup, our world environment and it is wired into our psyches. The lack of water can kill us. Hemingway soothed Nick Adam's troubled mind by exploring with him the waters of the Big Two-Hearted River near Seney, MI. Notwithstanding Paris' widely reputed beauty, Camus detested its grey, grim facades and equally grey weather. He celebrated the Mediterranean coast of his Algiers boyhood with an idealization of its beaches, sand and waters. And his near pagan worship of the sun and the sea as a life force for he and his poverty-stricken friends is evidenced amply in his work.

June 29, 2020

DAY 105

The Matanzas Pass Bridge connects San Carlos Island, home of the shrimp fleet, to Estero Island, aka Ft. Myers Beach. San Carlos is connected to the mainland by the San Carlos Bridge. The Little Carlos Bridge connects Estero Island at the south end to Bonita Springs. The Matanzas Pass Bridge, spanning the Intercoastal, is our focus today. It was built in 1979 replacing the colorful, but erratic swing bridge which had been around in various reincarnations since 1921. At its present height it is 70 feet above water and walking it back and forth it covers 1.39 miles. By the way, "Matanzas" means massacre. Probably involved Spanish soldiers and Calusa Indians. Joyce and I walk it every morning we are here.

Until you get your uphill and downhill legs under you it can be a shin splinting ordeal. For me, it takes a couple of days. Our best time ever was 20:30; today, our second day, 22:27. Just warming up. We never stop because we can get to our favorite dive bar, Bonito Bill's, faster for a cold one. Best done before 8:00 am when the temp is below 90 degrees.

Unfortunately, our friend Kim K's mother passed away on her 80th birthday.

The water in the Gulf is "blood warm."

June 30, 2020

DAY 106

Dinner with the kids…three pounds of shrimp and still not enough! Troubling incident, to me, occurred as we were walking from their unit to ours here at Lahaina Inn Resort. A guy who I have known for over thirty years was BBQing with his wife. I should have known better than bumping forearms with him since he just had open heart surgery a year ago. His wife was rightfully concerned and said: "get back, Rich!" Totally tone deaf on my part and very embarrassing. What was I thinking?

July 1, 2020

DAY 107

It is 4:05am and I made a big decision. I hope Joyce understands. My younger daughter Cam and her family are coming to the beach on Saturday. I have seen them twice before covid-19, but not Cait's. This week has been with them, enjoying them and seeing how the kids have grown and matured this past year. Even though I have already booked next week starting July 4th, I am going to leave Saturday and forfeit my rent. I am concerned and I want to be quarantined with Joyce in our own home.

Caitlen and Dave took Joyce and me out to dinner at South Beach Grill. Ate outside safely. Thanks so much, guys. It was delicious. Fettuccini in a broth that had spinach, tomato chips, spices and perfectly seared scallops and shrimp. Frog legs for lunch!

July 2, 2020

DAY 108

Cam and the kids have been at our house in Tarpon Springs this week. She was glad Joyce and I cancelled out. Got most of my week two money back, all but the deposit. If they rent it tomorrow for next week get that back, too. Wrote a poem:

> ESCAPE ROOM (Defeating death or trying to)
>
> Never a window unlatched
>
> Checked if hidden between open door and wall.
>
> Sealed "slip through" cracks on floor.
>
> Shoved bureaus over trap doors
>
> Caps on skylights.
>
> Still getting out, somehow.
>
> Or, if not,
>
> Etch ALMOST on my stone!

July 3, 2020

DAY 109

Well, it has come down to this. We are now the deplorables, the losers left behind, just like the Syrian refugees, and the Central American caravan. No one in the world wants us dropping by. We have been turned away by most European countries. We white guys landed on the east coast of this magnificent land in the early 1600s. Simultaneously, we began robbing and killing the Natives and establishing slavery as the national heritage for all to come. We moved to the Pacific coast, covering this huge land and making the moon our last frontier. Because of Trump, we have devolved into misplaced persons. We are once again expelled from the Garden. Irony is our bitter pill. We are our own "huddled masses yearning to breathe free." We are alone with our own stupidity. Whether we voted for Trump or have been accepting of his actions, we are all guilty because we allowed his election to happen. Our silence has lent credence to our cowardly elected officials. Blame them, if you will, but not entirely. They led where we let them go. There is only one moment left for redemption and that occurs on November 3, 2020.

July 4, 2020

DAY 110…Not much to celebrate. Even without the plague, our country stinks at the top!

Back from Ft. Myers Beach. It was wonderful seeing Cait, Dave, Owen and the kids. Yet the Covid-19 threat kept a constant damper on the vacation. As I mentioned, we cut our vacation a week short as we were anxious to get back home. Here is our new version of an old condition: the "Stockholm Syndrome for Quarantine." We only feel safe at home in our familiar and comfortable quarantine zone.

July 5, 2020

DAY 111

Enjoying the simple pleasures of home…our great mattress and a good night's sleep. Cooking a meal for us. Not much else to comment on.

July 6, 2020

DAY 112

Got a lot done this morning. Took a practically new fishing pole I am not using and shipped it via UPS to Jordan's Owen in Cincinnati. I had promised it to him. Something about that kid I love…his obvious intelligence, willingness to help, his respectfulness and his love and concern for his family. The young man was well brought up. Got my dinner prep from the grocery…stuffed peppers.

I had two phone conversations with Ron Stutzman, managing partner at Lahaina in Ft. Myers. He wondered if something was wrong that made us leave early? Assured him there was not a problem, just uneasy with the covid-19 exposure. He generously gave me a two/thirds return of my prepaid second week and then called later to say he rented the unit I owned for five days at $615.00 for me. Ron and I have been friends for thirty-seven years. He is fighting lung cancer. It will not be the same there without him if it worsens.

Extra bonus: We heard Bob Dylan's CD on the American Songbook. Loved "Be Beautiful," our next kitchen dance tune.

July 7, 2020

DAY 113

I am not sure I can ever celebrate July 4 again. As any thinking person knows, this country was founded on the extermination of Native Americans, slavery and the consistent use of force. Now we employ slightly more subtle techniques to keep many people down, politically, economically and socially. The current rot at the top of our government has worked its way through the body politic. Much of the world is onto our machinations. The Constitution, our protection, is being misused and abused. Money and power are the only measures of success. How long must one live to see this country put on the right path?

July 8, 2020

DAY 114

My niece Collyn Hawley and her husband Corey both have contracted Covid-19. Collyn got it from Corey. Their conditions unknown to me. (since have recovered). My brother may have contracted it. He was in Pidgeon Forge, Tennessee since Saturday or Sunday. He has been sick for three days. Symptoms are extreme fatigue, disorientation and a fever. I begged his wife to take him to the emergency room, but she might not. Says she is afraid to wake him. He must be tested. Hope he's OK, but I am worried.

July 9, 2020

DAY 115

My sister-in-law took Tom to a clinic last night. He got tested, results in five days. Symptoms: fatigue, high temperature, disorientation, high blood pressure and poor oxygen to blood ratio. All the symptoms, it seems to me, but the test result will tell the story. The nurse who brought him back to the car said: "you have a very sick man." At 73, this is a hazardous situation. Will keep in touch with them.

July 10, 2020

DAY 116

About three days to go for Tom's test results. Sue said he seemed a little better this morning and was hungry. Still a temperature of 102.5 last night. Joyce, my sister, called her last night and told her that my nephew's ashes were inserted into a wall somewhere with only the immediate family and a priest present. They have closed ranks like the KGB and the rest of us are left guessing as to the cause of his death. To me, that is not something for idle speculation.

Talked to my friend and former colleague Pat Savage yesterday about figuring out a way to get to Ireland. Pat has an Irish passport and is applying for citizenship, but if he goes, he still must quarantine for 14 days. He is no better off than me, assuming I could even find a plane to take us. It was good talking to a friend I made 51 years ago. Among Pat's many accomplishments, one stood out to me. He searched in Ireland for the grave of Mike Tarpey, an Irish colleague of ours, found it in a rainstorm and had a drink of Irish on the spot. Then he texted me what he had done.

July 11, 2020

DAY 117

Just talked to Tom and he got his test results…negative! Now the question is what caused this severe and painful illness? He has sleep apnea and a troubled sinus system. I recommended he mention Symbicort to his doctor and possibly get a script for it. It certainly works for me…no asthma and no snoring! Funny… if it had been covid-19, he would be over it. The test simply shows that you can still get it! Am questioning the test's validity. It seems more than coincidental that one could be sick with the same symptoms as the plague and not have the plague! Tests are not 100% certain.

Hooked up on FB with a former student, Steve Frankel, who is now a professor (PhD, U. of Chicago) at my alma mater Xavier University.

Delicious frozen margaritas and vegetable quesadillas tonight!

July 12, 2020

DAY 118

If a paradox is a seemingly contradictory or absurd statement that, upon examination, is found to be true, then I wish to posit a new fallacy, the "untrue" paradox, based on the reality of Covid-19.

Every nation/state needs a robust economy. (true) The USA needs an economy re-opened. (true) To do this, we need workers back on their jobs.

(true) If workers are to be back on their jobs, they need schools re-opened to safely contain their kids. (true) But many workers are at risk going back to jobs in confined and crowded transportation and work areas. Children must be store housed in schools with poorly prepared instructional areas, perhaps only a cut above the caged kids on the border. Teachers and staff are endangered, as well. Because of this, more of our population will be in even greater jeopardy.

Most people in this economy are not self-employed. They work for salaries however big or small. Why is there a loud demand for them to return and put themselves in danger? It is only partially to pay the rent and put food on the table. Basically, the real "need" is for the 1% to continue to amass fortunes at the workers' expense. Prior to the plague, this reality was generally ignored. Now to allow this demand to be fulfilled, children must be placed in contagious "kid storage" under the guise of education. They become an essential sacrificial link in this saga of greed. It is all of one piece.

I have said before that after each cataclysmic event in human history large changes come about and I believe our economy and the distribution of wealth will be changed radically. Trump is not the root cause of these inequalities, but his miserable public statements denying science and his desperate and doomed re-election strategies have brought them to the fore.

July 13, 2020

DAY 119

I mentioned before I was reading the latest Scott Turow courtroom novel entitled *The Last Trial*. It goes without saying that his work makes understandable
the complexities of trial procedures and the deftness of his plot structure and
his characterizations leaves John Grisham's work fit for middle school readers.
Scott Turow lived not many miles from me in Chicago's northern suburbs, but
light years away in terms of prestigious real estate. However, I once came in close
contact with him. He and my wife had both ruptured their appendixes on the
same day. We rushed her to Evanston Hospital from Skokie. They immediately
prepared her for surgery and when I next saw her, I was standing alongside her
gurney waiting for her to be dispatched to an operating room. Foot to head with
her in the corridor was the author himself! Off they went and I was left with an
angry Mrs. Turow. It seemed they had tickets to fly to Bimini in the next couple
of days and she was upset with his "lack of internal planning." She explained this
dilemma to me in no uncertain terms. It was too late to cancel the trip, but the
enterprising Mrs. Turow asked me if I wanted to buy their two tickets. That was
my wife they just wheeled in, I said. I would go with you, but I have the kids at
home. Ignoring my humor, she stomped off to the waiting room. I made sure I
found another one.

July 14, 2020

DAY 120 (Bastille Day)

We watched that wonderful 1935 Selznick film version of Dicken's *A Tale of Two Cities* starring Ronald Coleman as Sydney Carton. I taught the novel many times and never tired of it. What I find marvelously insidious was Sydney's note to Lucie written in her husband Charles' hand and delivered to her pinned to the coat of the drugged Charles! Sydney reminds her that he is carrying out the promise he made to her years before, that is, he will do anything to save a life of one she loves! The immediate relevance to her must be overwhelming. She has her husband safe and sound, but can she look upon him the same as before? Charles has been nothing but well-meaning trouble. He leaves the peasants for whom he professes loyalty and his abandonment of Gabelle, his tutor and father figure, was wrong. By going back to France for Gabelle at the worst possible time he endangers his whole family! Sydney saved him in London on the charges of treason. Dr. Manette almost saves him in the French trial. Carton again saves him by taking his place on death row and having Charles smuggled out. Sydney has placed himself deeply in Lucie's (un?) conscious mind, through the letter, as a constant reminder to her of her husband's weaknesses and his (Sydney's) eternal love. Charles has a difficult road ahead once this all sinks in with Lucie. The note is a time bomb that explodes in his face every time she reads it…which I think will be often over the years.

July 15, 2020

DAY 121

Little Jeffie Sessions, formerly the cutest ears in the Senate, the Pixie from Dixie, was defeated last night in the Alabama Republican primary by Tommy Tuberville, Auburn's former head coach. Trump's endorsement of TT did the little fella' in. Tuberville may beat Doug Jones in the election in November. He then will become the most ill-prepared man to enter the Senate since Bill Scott of Virginia, who once mistook grain silos for missile silos and the Persian Gulf for the Suez Canal.

It appears now that Jeffie and Ma Sessions will retire to the porch of their Beauregard, AL plantation and drink sweet tea!

Oh, snap! I completely forgot! Taxes today? I thought...never mind, already paid them! Like a guy just said on tv: so glad my tax dollars will be gobbled up in small business loans to real estate developers, big chains, the Catholic Church and an assorted group of other one per centers!

July 16, 2020

DAY 122

Tom update…My younger brother Tom may be the first person in the world who had Covid-19 symptoms but did not have Covid-19! After a seven hour hospital stay attended by an infectious disease doctor, it was determined that he had a severe urinary tract infection brought about by poison ivy. It appears he contracted the poison ivy on his hands while he was gardening and then relieved himself and, apparently, held on too long! I refrained from comment, but finally asked if he had been gardening naked? A friend of ours recommended that he wear latex gloves in the future while urinating!

Trump has sunk to a new depth, but it is still early. Starting today, all coronavirus statistics, new cases and deaths especially, will go directly to the White House, via the HHS, bypassing the CDC. Most news outlets report that the pandemic will probably end with an announcement tomorrow!

Remember…with Trump, whatever day it is, the next day will be worse!

July 17, 2020

DAY 123

We are going to Lee County tomorrow to pick up our dog, Casey! He is a seven years old rescue Lhasa Apso. They originated in Tibet and his breed was developed by Buddhist monks as monastery sentinels. Maybe we can meditate together! Had the same breed years ago and she was the best dog. Expect the male to be a tad feistier. Cannot wait to get him home. Quarantine demands diversion!

July 18, 2020

DAY 124

Following the death of the great Congressman John Lewis, a near martyr at Selma, AL, and during the absolute horror of roaming, unmarked "lawmen" pulling citizens off the streets of Portland, Casey joined our family. He might be the most lovable thing we have known in a long time. After a drive to Ft. Myers, we finally had the meet up with him and his foster mom. We were anxious as parents meeting their daughter or son's intended. What if he does not respond to us and Doreen says, "not a good match." But she didn't and even said: "You do want him, don't you?" Of course, we did! Could not write that check for him fast enough and buy him the most expensive dog bed on the planet! He slept on it all the way home then woke and started warming up to Joyce's advances. He sniffed the house thoroughly, did his business outdoors about three times, ate his dinner and slept like a log through the night in our bedroom. At one point, he followed me to the front door when I left for the grocery. She told me he laid down on the floor and waited until I got back. He loves chucking under his chin, having his ears itched as well as his ruff. He needs his long nails trimmed as he has little purchase on the wood floors which cause an endearing shuffle. He is a Lhasa Apso combined with some guy on the street, and we love every inch of him. Our job is to see that this poor, thrice uprooted guy has the best final home he deserves.

July 19, 2020

DAY 125

I think Casey has a bad hip. Get him to the vet this week. He seems to be feeling more and more comfortable here…sniffing from room to room. Loves lap sitting and falls asleep quickly. We were sitting in the living room talking and he was lying on the floor at about 9:30 pm. He got up, stretched and went to bed! Maybe bored? Cracked me up. He loves that bed. Not even Archie Sussex has a bed that good! Split pea soup, baguettes and blueberry cobbler for dinner. Big workout today. Am exhausted. Night, all.

July 20, 2020

DAY 126

Well, this was Casey's first full day home and he seems to love it. What he really likes is going for walks, four of them by my count. He does his business each time! Wore himself out, though. At 9:00pm he was asleep in Joyce's lap. I picked him up and carried him to his bed. He never woke up.

This was Joyce's favorite dinner night…roasted veggies. OK, I cheated a bit. After I put the dog to bed, I had two hot dogs! I like roasted asparagus, carrots, peppers, onions, squash and zucchini plus a sweet potato, but it still was not quite enough.

July 21, 2020

DAY 126

This morning revealed an interesting fact. In three short days Joyce noted that Casey has taken on my persona. He gets up at 7:00am with me. I take him out for a quick pee. He comes in and eats his breakfast, and then, goes back to bed! My boy! Just like me! I believe in a psychiatric condition known as "folie a deux!" This condition exists when two people live with each other and one is nuts. The other will gradually acquire the same delusional attributes. Think Kim K and Kanye!

Yearly cancer checkup or as I like to think of it…the bladder invasion! Couple of tense moments when Marty Richmond, MD discovers some inflammation. Some blood samples taken. He will get back to me whether they are benign or not. Then he goes to his computer, prints out a sheet and tells me everything is OK. Long, tedious session, but over for another year.

Dog shopping for a new halter, leash, food and a brush. Closing in on $500 for this rescue. I do not care! He is already priceless!

The redoubtable Long Tom (my baby brother) is on the mend!

July 22, 2020

Day 127

Back on the heavy bag for a brief workout today. Seems my right wrist is healed up from some inflammation, probably arthritis.

I was listening to some dumbass Covid-19 responses in Florida and Alabama concerning the wearing of masks and congregating in groups. No need to repeat them, except for this classic: "We have been cooped up for three or four months! We deserve to go out and party with our friends!" Reminds me of when we were kids up north and the first warm day of Spring arrived after a long miserable winter. We ripped off our winter coats and ran and biked and played outside for hours! Then we all caught colds and were sick for a few days. These guys run slightly bigger risks than that.

July 23, 2020

DAY 128

I finished Hillary Mantel's final novel, *The Mirror & The Light*, of her trilogy based upon Thomas Cromwell, advisor to Henry 8th, and former mentee of Cardinal Wolsey. The first two books are *Wolf Hall* and *Bringing Up the Bodies*. From this reading, I have become curious about Wolsey and his downfall which led me to Shakespeare's *Henry 8th*. Wolsey's fall from grace as Henry's principal advisor and his admonition to Cromwell are detailed in Act III. ii. His replacement will be Thomas More who, in turn, will be brought down by Thomas Cromwell. As with all those close to Henry, including his wives, Cromwell will lose his head at the end of *The Mirror & The Light*.

Cardinal Wolsey to Cromwell:

Mark but my fall and that that ruined me.

Cromwell, I charge thee, fling away ambition:

By that sin fell the angels; how can man, then,

The image of his Maker, hope to win by it?

Love thyself last; cherish those hearts that hate thee.

Corruption wins not more than honesty.

Still in thy right hand carry gentle peace,

To silence envious tongues. Be just, and fear not:

Let all the ends thou aim at be thy countries,

Thy God's and truth's: then if thou fall

Thou fall a blessed martyr!

O CROMWELL, CROMWELL!

HAD I BUT SERVED MY GOD WITH HALF THE ZEAL

I SERVED MY KING, HE WOULD NOT IN MINE AGE

HAVE LEFT ME NAKED TO MINE ENEMIES.

(magnificent words by the Bard for Wolsey's character)

July 24, 2020

DAY 129

Trying not to concentrate too much on the news of the day because I assume most folks pay attention and do not need my "expertise." However, yesterday's takedown of Rep. Ted Yoho, aka #floridaman, by AOC was stunning. She told this trump wannabe that he had given males everywhere permission to use abusive language, for example, "you fucking bitch," on his own wife and daughters. That she is intelligent is a given, but her ability to think on her feet and deliver is likewise incredible. N.B. "Christian" Ted has since been removed from the board of a Christian Food provider.

My brother's infection is cleared up! Almost three weeks of illness.

July 25, 2020

DAY 130

Talked to my friend Dawn Marks today and heard some shattering news. Before we moved here, almost eighteen years ago, she and Bud, who had bought a resort on Clearwater Beach, provided us with much needed information. They suggested their real estate man and his daughter to find us our house, likewise their lawyer and their tax accountant. Since we have shared the same lawyer and, as I have mentioned previously, he died suddenly on February 15th, I asked if she had a new lawyer? She did and was glad to get him. Then she told me that our mutual lawyer John Martin had committed suicide. He probably had bilked a couple of dozen real estate clients to the tune of millions of dollars. An investor had called him demanding his escrowed five million dollars and said he was coming to the office for it immediately. John shot himself in his office, leaving a wife and four kids. It had been in the local papers which I rarely read.

So trite to say, but does anyone ever know anyone else? I knew the man for eight years and trusted him implicitly. He did good work for me and hand carried me through setting up a trust for me and my daughters after their mother's death. I told my girls if anything happened to me, John would guide them through the trust. If he would have suggested investing with him, I would have surely considered it. The last time we saw him he drew up a similar trust for Joyce and her daughters. She thought he was delightful. How could he carry on daily being so thoughtful and professional with this stuff on his mind? (see April 8th entry again for my initial thoughts on this gentleman)

July 26, 2020

DAY 131

Thomas Merton wrote in *Conjectures of a Guilty Bystander* that the Dalai Lama was so lonely as a child that he used to climb to the roof of his palace and study the neighboring houses with binoculars to watch people having fun at outdoor parties. Word got around that he did this, so people stopped having outdoor parties in order not to sadden him further.

July 27, 2020

DAY 132

Casey's first visit to the vet went well. Nothing serious…dry eyes cleaned, cluttered ears reamed out and toenails clipped.

July 28, 2020

DAY 133

I am studying a colorful and persuasive brochure from Book Baby publishing company. I still have five months to go. What to do with this mélange of facts and opinions? To Be Determined!

Inventoried our library shelves this morning. Between us we own 845 books and add to that every week. We want to reach at least a thousand. We are inspired by so many library shelves behind speakers on television every day!

July 29, 2020

DAY 134

From my comfortable position on the quarantine sidelines...retired, tested, adequate income, grown children and a wife and dog I love to be with...I am reduced to observation and opinion, often even based on facts! I hesitate to ever call myself an atheist simply because it is too tedious to explain. Just say I am a non-believer in prayer, divine intervention and an afterlife. What I do love are the words of Jesus in the New Testament...those beatitudes delivered in the Sermon on the Mountain. Whether Jesus existed or not is immaterial. The words he said or those attributed to him by some ancient writer are a blueprint for living. In our time, do those who "hunger and thirst for justice," those who are the "peacemakers," those who are "persecuted for righteousness sake" attain these ends? Or do they "mourn" without comfort? (continued)

July 30, 2020

DAY 135

Is it just me being fashionably cynical or has Christianity taken a 360 degree turn toward the worse? True, many denominations still provide institutional charity, but have its' members forgotten or even learned the admonitions of Jesus? After listening to the Gospel on Sunday, how hateful folks can become at a moment's notice. How hardened they react in the face of another's loss. How can we not accept any guilt for slavery and the loss of black lives through the ages and to the present day? It is our national "original sin" and, until it is acknowledged, it will continue to torment us. This problem is ongoing, along with lying politicians, hatred of immigrants and the LGBTQ community, politics of division, white privilege and white supremacy, unfair distribution of income and the constant exploitation of the poor. Sadly, there is no end in sight!

July 31, 2020

DAY 136

From a FB posting of a note that needed to be rewritten in the following context. Parentheses indicate the original wording.

Dear Christians, (LBGTQ community)

If you do not want to be treated differently for being Christian (gay), then stop acting like being Christian (gay) somehow makes you special. Your religion (gayness) is neither an achievement nor a holiday. You have not accomplished anything simply by being a Christian (gay).

August 1, 2020

When Trump is accused of neglecting Covid-19, the statements that follow usually are prefaced with "Trump didn't cause Covid-10, but…" Well, he did cause the death of Herman Cain, former presidential candidate. Cain was a Trump surrogate. He ran something called Blacks for Trump. He signed the waiver and attended the rally at Tulsa, OK. Whatever this man, who had serious medical issues, thought about mask wearing, I do not know. But he did not wear one to avoid offending Trump. Call it karma, irony or just bad judgement for following Trump's nuttiness, he died three weeks later. Without sarcasm, I say RIP, Godfather Pizza Man.

Trump raises election delay possibility in total contradiction of the Constitution of the United States. Nothing has ever delayed or cancelled the presidential election in this country. Not even world wars. Only Congress can do so and they never have. This latest madness bears out the fact that he has no election strategy short of lying, cheating and causing chaos and confusion.

August 2, 2020

DAY 138

Beginning today, there are ninety-five days until the presidential election on November 3. If you are not registered, get so! If you forget to vote for Biden, I will come to wherever you are and you will have to deal with me! Simple as that. This is the most important election in the history of elections!

August 3, 2020

DAY 139

Some bits of information: the actor Wilfred Brimley, dead at the age of 85. He played Pop Fisher, manager of the Knights and its' star player Roy Hobbs in the film *The Natural*. "Hobbs' get a bat!" "Red, why can't I get a decent drink of water in this dugout?" Who can ever forget his world-weary portrayal:" Red, my mother told me to be a farmer!" No one could ignore him in *Cocoon*! Ironically enough, he was 20 years younger than his fellow actors in the film. Forty-nine years of age at that time.

Nancy Pelosi, an old master at the art of the political takedown, worked some sleight of hand the other day. Merely attacking Trump for disinformation would probably have little effect, so she attacked Dr. Birx by saying she was ineffective, never contradicted Trump and supplied him with bad information. Hoping that Birx would defend herself and her reputation by blaming Trump, she would reveal, if indirectly, that he constructs his own inane theories and conspiracies. Did not quite work but it did force Birx to come out the next day with her most truthful and accurate statement about the pandemic, "It is extraordinarily widespread." This, in a complete contradiction of Trump! Unfortunately for Brix, a newcomer to "gotcha'" politics, a tweet landed her on the bench for being forthcoming!

Tropical storm Isaias appears to be sparing poor old, beat up Florida!

August 4, 2020
DAY 140

Once more the teachers are put upon to a ridiculous extent! In Hillsborough County, where I worked for the union, the teachers will be responsible for the cleaning materials and cleaning protocol in the classroom when on-site schooling begins. Not to mention handwashing lessons and mask wearing procedures instructions for all kids! What more can be asked of school employees, even in this pandemic? Already they are responsible not only for a kid's academics, but for his/her socialization skills, nutrition, driving skills, summer programs and physical activities. Why are the public schools, among the more fragile entities in society, always called upon to do the near impossible? When desegregation was instituted, of course, the schools carried it out. Why was not the army or navy, police or firemen or a myriad of government departments used for this task? I strongly suspect the docility of teachers was a major consideration. I recommend that schools close on-site operations until at least January and then re-assess this precarious situation. E-learning should get the proper funding and teacher training necessary to carry on education at a safe distance or the teachers and staff should refuse to participate!

Cortisone shot for Casey today. Turns out he is a paw licker. Probably an allergy condition is causing this. We are so happy that little rescue Casey has Dr. Byron Hassell as a neighbor!!

August 5, 2020

My dad's birthday was today. He was born in 1903. He and my mother were married on this day in 1937.

I have always been fascinated by General Douglas MacArthur. I was born at the inception of WWII and entered the first grade at its' end. The war dominated my earliest years. Eisenhower, Patton, Marshall were household names to us, but Mac was special to me. I had a statue of him, complete with corncob pipe and sunglasses, on my chest of drawers. Much later, I read about him in William Manchester's "American Caesar" and found out some amazing facts! As one critic said: "Listen to the best things about him and the worst things about him. They are all true!" Apart from his many controversies and magisterial ego, Douglas MacArthur, the American Caesar, the Shogun, was idolized by the very people he defeated. It is a fact that MacArthur in 1947, aided by two lawyer officers, wrote the constitution for the Japan that he defeated and reconstructed. It is still in effect as I write! Please note, this conservative military man signed off on the following articles:

Article 15…Universal suffrage

Article 19…Freedom of religion

Article 23…Academic freedom guaranteed

Article 26…Free compulsory education

Article 28…The right of workers to organize and bargain collectively guaranteed. (my favorite!)

August 6, 2020…DAY 142

Covid-19 hits my family. All of us will experience this plague, directly or indirectly, eventually!

Even though she wore latex gloves, a mask and worked outdoors as a waitress, my granddaughter, Jordan Leigh Sweeney, contracted Covid-19. She is isolated at her father's house and her two brothers will stay with their mother to avoid contact. Everyone in both my daughters' families are quickly being retested. She graduated from the University of Dayton in May. We had concocted a plan. She would work at a sports bar and make some money this summer and, as a graduation gift, I would send her to Europe in the Fall. She could pursue a career job when she returned. Covid-19 stopped that plan, but she worked anyway. She has lost her senses of taste and smell.

August 7, 2020

DAY 143

Joyce and I had lunch yesterday with Dawn at Parker Manor, catching up and seeing how she is doing after Bud's death.

Jonathon Swan's Axios interview with Trump continues to dominate the news. Our President's ignorance is abysmal, yet he effectively spins non-facts and outright lies into "truths" for his base. A good percentage of them believes Dr. Fauci works for the Democrat Party and is lying to America! Never have I seen or heard in my politically aware life anyone like Trump.

As one Twitter critic said: "The Axios interview is one cognitive test Trump failed."

Fajitas tonight! "Yo Adrian," No! "Yo Semite!" Trump's garbled pronunciation of "Yosemite!"

August 8, 2020

DAY 144

I am seriously concerned about the situation in my daughter's family. My oldest granddaughter, as mentioned earlier, has tested positive for Covid-19. She is isolated from the family, but did she start soon enough? Her family consist of two forty-year old adults, and a thirteen, eleven and a three-year old. The baby is the problem. If Julia has it, then everyone has it because she is constantly fussed over, kissed, picked up and played with by the others. She will be tested today by her pediatrician with results available immediately. Everyone else awaits their results in the slow lane. Same with my other daughter who lives close by. Her kids have been tested and await results, except the oldest, Emlyn, who has Type One diabetes. She will be tested today by her endocrinologist with the result known immediately. I am extremely anxious for these results.

August 9, 2020

Day 145

Julia has tested negative which probably takes Cait, Dave, James and John off the hook, but we will wait for their results. I am concerned for Emmy who was tested yesterday with supposed instant results. However, no word is yet forthcoming. I hope to hear soon.

Hillsborough County teachers got a setback late yesterday. The plan that the School Board released was for e-learning and closed buildings for the first four weeks beginning August 24th. The plan has been rejected by the Florida Department of Education. Basically, the Governor and the Education Commissioner are saying that each school needs to submit a plan for why they cannot reopen or face withheld funding. Without a special exemption, brick and mortar building must be available for classes five days a week.

Hillsborough teachers and staff have difficult choices. Traditionally, since 1968, the teachers have fallen back on the assumption that any job action could cost them their jobs, a loss of instructional credentials and pensions. If they choose to maintain their health and their lives, they believe that these losses are a given. If they would just stand together, state-wide, none of these things could be put into effect!

The school district I taught in for 32 years has gone to e-learning for the entire first semester. In brief, classroom instruction is not an option. Each student receives a free chrome book. What the teachers and staff think, I do not know, but everyone is, at least in theory, safe from Covid-19 at school.

State by state, even district by district, the immediate future of education is governed by either safety and common sense or a desire to appease the lunatic in the White House.

August 9, 2020

DAY 146

Florida Governor Ron DeSantis has a thuggish demeanor when he is pressured. He angrily carries out the school opening wishes of Trump with an obviously conflicted mind. If Trump goes in November, where is this "good" soldier left? In a complete rejection of reasonable scientific input, the Governor has silenced County Health Doctors and reduced them to "advisory" status. They cannot state outright that a school district should remain opened or closed under pain of dismissal. Emlyn, my granddaughter, has not yet received her test results. Everyone is on hold except Jordan (positive) and the youngest, Julia (negative).

Let us not even go to Sturgis, ND, literally or in any other way. It is plainly and simply a gathering of idiots! Leave them to their own devices and karma and stay way clear!

August 10, 2020
DAY 147

Latest word from my kids in suburban Chicago on the Covid-19 situation. My eleven years old grandson, John, tested positive, but shows no symptoms, at least yet. Should hear results for everyone else sometime today. All were told to wait until John finishes his quarantine to be tested again.

Cameron and her kids, Emmy, Avery and Owen have all tested negative.

August 11, 2020
DAY 148

There is a marvelous book I read in 2017 and recalled today. *The Journey Home*, by Irish author Dermot Bolger, explores the economic wreckage of Ireland and the effect on its' youth in the '70s. "We (the young characters) came from nowhere and found we belonged nowhere else." Unlike John Wayne's escape home to Ireland after a personal tragedy in *The Quiet Man*, "these kids have a free-floating nostalgia and yearnings for times unknown, before they were born, that seem as indelible as original sin."

"Home was not the place where you were born but the place you created for yourself, where you did not need to explain, where you finally became what you were."

To me, this quote seemed so true. Being raised at home by my parents was fine as far as being provided for, but it was a constant game of withholding myself concerning sex, dubious friends and thoughts about the future. They never really knew what I was thinking or even doing. And they rarely asked. Where then was home? Maybe it was away at college where I could be myself and not have to explain even my most absurd statements and actions. It could be at that place where I became self-aware enough to realize my follies and ignorance and either alter them or accept myself for what I was or probably both.

Home: the place we create for ourselves! I do not think it is exactly like Robert Frost framed it in his narrative poem "The Death of the Hired Man:" "Home is the place where, when you have to go there, / They have to take you in." At least, not for the young people in this novel.

August 12, 2020

Day 149

Washed the lanai windows and cleaned the deck and the furniture yesterday. Kamala Harris chosen by Joe Biden as his running mate. First woman of color to play such a role. So much being said about this pick! Joe fulfilled his promise which is a good first step. Today's campaign rollout was a huge success!

Went to the Urgent Care Unit today and got a splint on the little finger of my right hand. It is probably broken, but the x-ray showed considerable arthritis which clouded the image. Cannot really pinpoint the cause but possibly attribute it to hitting the big bag.

Its' been six years yesterday since Robin Williams died. There is not an English teacher who saw *Dead Poet's Society* who would not wish for a few Mr. Keating moments in his/her career! The man ignored curriculum and freelanced his way through every class and in his off-hours! If only one's "real" teaching life resembled the movie.

August 13, 2020

DAY 150

FOO-TIL- ITIES... a new pronunciation by our esteemed President...of Fatalities. One of his many strange enunciations.

The best toast in the world comes from the bread made at La Segunda Bakery in Ybor City. It is not a Cuban baguette, but rather a circular sliced loaf. You must cut a large slice in half to fit it in the toaster. It is well worth the effort.

There is much speculation about Kamala Harris eating Mike Pence alive in the Vice-Presidential Debate. Fiery Kamala will ignore Pence and go after Trump directly. If Joe faltered on a response in his debate, she is there to cover for him. Pence will be the lame surrogate trying to explain Trump. She will attack, allow him a few seconds to respond and then attack again.

I think the rollout went exceptionally well yesterday. Joe kept his gaffe-free speech to nineteen minutes and Harris jammed a world of introduction and critique into fifteen minutes.

August 14, 2020

DAY 151

167,253 (a number that grows daily) persons are dead of the novel corona virus in the USA since January 21, 2020. This is the very virus that our president termed a "hoax," and ignored. This same president argued with plague experts, said it would vanish in the heat of summer, mocked efforts to mitigate it and, finally, chose to simply ignore it. "Open businesses, return to jobs, play baseball and football, start school in buildings," he said. If he was a man of conscience and empathy who had temporarily lost his perspective, these words of Macbeth, a murderer who can't shake his guilt, would be readily understandable to Trump: "O, full of scorpions is my mind/...I am in blood/Stepped in so far, that should I wade no more,/Returning were as tedious as going o'er." But they cannot register a shred of regret or remorse in this man.

He is what we citizens must cope with on this day in America. Our country is slipping away.

Oh, this just in! #URINETROUBLETRUMP (See Michael Cohen's book, "Disloyal.")

August 15, 2020

Day 152

My brother-in-law Jack Brosseit, "Action Jack" to his many Arizona fans, received some interesting information recently. My daughter Cameron told me that in a circuitous way, via 23 and Me, a young woman in Oklahoma discovered that Jack is her father. Somehow, through those many DNA "relatives" they match with a person, she finally got the truth from her mother that "yep, he is your daddy." Both married mom and unmarried Jack were American Airlines flight attendants working together at the time. Jack has been married for years to my late wife's younger sister and is the father of my two nieces. According to Cameron, who got the news from her cousin, the new addition is a fortyish artist with her own studio in Oklahoma. A similar situation occurred to a friend of mine in Tampa this past year. He is happily reunited with his daughter who has been readily accepted by his family.

August 16, 2020

DAY 153

I neglected to mention yesterday day that it was the Feast of the Assumption into heaven of the Virgin Mary. In my usual state of non-observing it would have passed right by, but two years ago today we went to mass in Florence because Joyce had never attended one in Italy. The church is the Monastery of San Marco at the head of the Via Cavour which runs past the Medici Palace to the historic district of the Duomo. This is the former home of Fra Angelico who painted a meditative scene in every cell for the edification of the monks and home also to the notorious monk, Savonarola, of "Bonfire of the Vanities" fame. If one really wants to get down with the Ascension, visit Titian's masterpiece of Mary's take-off for home at the Friari Dei Glorioso in Venice.

We took the amazing Casey the Wonder Dog for a walk today. I usually handle the first outing of the day as it is time for his manly act upon awakening. Joyce follows suit later. Often two or three times later! Today I went on their walk! He was stunned when all three of us left together. "Wait a sec! What is Jim doing here? Oh, the car!" He went to the car and would not leave. "Jim never walks! He sits in a chair or drives the car! He is not in his chair…ergo. I love riding in the car!" It took us a few minutes to get those legs moving up the walk!

August 17, 2020

Day 154

Empathy Analysis Day

As everyone knows and as every disclaimer "disclaims" before criticizing a person, no one can really tell what is in another's mind. let us consider the President's actions in the last few days. His younger brother was hospitalized Friday night, reportedly, in grave condition. I am sure that members of his immediate family were in attendance. The President got to his side late Saturday afternoon. Robert Trump died on Saturday night. It was written that President Trump "appeared to have been crying when he later exited his plane." Okay... pretty darn normal! It almost makes a Trump hater cut him some slack. "Maybe he feels things just like I do." Biden and his wife sent a sincere message of consolation as did Harris. Then the bottom fell out of this mini era of good feeling. Pictures reveal Trump playing golf all of Saturday afternoon and laughing it up with his partner just after. He then roars off to the hospital, bids his brother god speed, and rushes back to Bedminster to catch his chopper home for a good night's sleep. Come on, man! At least he did not sleep with a hooker at this significant moment. Don's last words about his brother are rather telling: "He was never jealous of me and all my accomplishments...#1 rated TV show, great real estate deals, the Presidency..."

August 18, 2020

The virtual Democrat Convention began last night. Read about Michelle Obama's speech, watch a repeat if you can, and then understand the power of her statement: "It is what it is."

Yesterday our little Casey had a rough go. Like new parents everywhere we experiment with our first dog together. If he likes to ride in the car like we think he does, then he will enjoy a lengthy ride to a specialist I had to see. Joyce went along with a book and her phone to sit with him in the car while I waited for my appointment…interminably! She walked him, gave him water and let him do his business. When I finally came back to the car, Joyce got out from behind the wheel to give me the driver's seat. We were both momentarily out of the car and Casey shrieked repeatedly. We have never heard him even bark. I thought his leash was caught, but his harness is nowhere near his throat. He was having a panic attack! He could not stop shaking and Joyce held him all the way home. (continued tomorrow)

August 19, 2020

DAY 156

No sooner then we got home, thunder and lightning started. Like most dogs, he reacted painfully, pacing randomly and shuddering. We took turns holding him in our laps and comforting him. Finally, this rugged day ended with him in his bed. Same thing happened again just last evening, and he ended up in our bed, snuggling as close as he could. I find his fright almost as painful as he does. We are reminded by these incidents of what a responsibility a little animal is. We welcomed him into our house and eagerly look after him. He provides us the opportunity to perform a dimension of care which is beneficial to our wellbeing, too.

August 20, 2020

DAY 157

I think Joe Biden nailed his acceptance speech last night wrapping up a successful democrat convention. Who would have guessed it could be pulled off virtually? Quite a feat of technology and people power, timing and organization.

I talked to my granddaughter Emmy, a high school sophomore, about her English assignment. She must read *Macbeth, Fahrenheit 451 and Mice and Men*. Asked me for help! Cannot wait to dig into those works with her! Regarding *Fahrenheit 451*, author Ray Bradbury was born 100 years ago in Waukegan, IL just a few miles down Grand Ave. from where she lives. The Ray Bradbury Experience Museum in Waukegan is at 13 N. Genesee St. 60085.

August 21, 2020

Day 158

Two dear friends and former teaching colleagues, Chris Kohl Beeftink and Dan Montgomery, both referenced on Facebook Joe Biden's quote of Irish poet Seamus Heaney in his nomination acceptance speech: "...our moment to make hope and history rhyme." Chris also mentioned that Biden in his youth read the poet Yeats' work aloud to help alleviate his stuttering.

I responded with a favorite line or two from Heaney's poem *Digging*: "By God, the old man could handle a spade./Just like his old man...But I've no spade to follow men like them…Between my finger and my thumb/The squat pen rests,/I'll dig with it."

And I added a story about Yeats that I heard in Dublin four years ago: The poet had never been in a pub. A friend took him to one. He sat down, ordered a small sherry and took a couple of sips. So, this is a pub," he said and then got up and left!

August 22, 2020
DAY 159

I have been running behind on my journal entries. As I mentioned before in this current charged atmosphere of politics, protest and Covid-19, I have no dog in the fight, no skin in the game. Therefore, I have been doing a bit of research and putting my results on Facebook. For the past two days I provided the reasons why we vote on a Tuesday in November and today I explained the make-up and role of the electoral college to be followed tomorrow by an analysis of the "swing" states. Both the voting dates and electoral college were arrived at out of necessity with plenty of quirky overtones.

August 23, 2020

DAY 160

Casey has abandoned his bed, the most expensive dog bed in the world. Queen Elizabeth's corgis would die for it, as would little Archie Sussex. He now has chosen to sleep on our bedroom floor on my golf blanket. All day he strutted around in his stylish thunder shirt which Joyce ordered for him. This wraparound garment keeps him from shaking when it thunders. Dogs can hear twice as good as humans. Even distant thunder affects them. The sudden drop in barometric pressure as a storm approaches, coupled with atomically charged molecules of static electricity, makes them shiver and shake. The sudden darkness frightens them, too. Our little guy immediately runs to whoever is nearest when it storms and wants to be picked up and soothed. The thunder shirt fits snuggly around him like a stroking pair of hands. However, it has not been tested in an all-out thunder boomer! He is keeping his paws crossed.

August 24, 2020

Written late. I am proud to say that today I never turned on the shitshow of a convention or never tuned into a word of analysis. I do know that the Republicans, for the first time in their party history, had no platform. No Party Platform! This is the list of aspirations, seldom fully met, but always ideals for which to be striven. Instead, they capitulated to Trump and his agenda for a second term for which an agenda does not exist! Chancellor Trump takes over just like another chancellor in 1933. I forget his name. This is not my America! My country more resembles the shattered Weimar Republic of 1933. Sickness and unemployment reign, death and division are everywhere.

August 25, 2020

DAY 162

A happy day! Joyce and I have been together four years today! When I met her my wife had passed away two and a half years before. After a couple of false starts in the interim, I just about had resigned myself to playing golf every day, eating out and drinking myself to sleep at night. Might sound good to some guys, but I got tired of it fast. I saw her picture on a dating sight. She was at dinner, kind of leaning forward and laughing at something somebody said. She was so cute... what the hell would she see in me? We met at Bahama Breeze and seemed to relate well. "Relate well!" I thought she was so attractive, and I could not believe she would want to see me again! We exchanged numbers and two nights later she was at my house. We have rarely been apart since then! Just this morning, we laughed thinking about our reactions if someone had said then "try lockdown for 162 days and see how cute you think each other is!"

I paraphrased some lines from a song we like and wrote these words in a card for her: "And since you are mine/I will never let you go/And that would be but beautiful I know."

August 26, 2020

DAY 163

228 students kicked out of Ohio State, and school has not even started, for crowded partying in campus neighborhoods. Go Bucks! Hey, no football!! Got to do something!

Pinellas County, FL, where we live, announced a 55% reduction in Covid-19 cases in the recent past. Florida is trending down, according to RT Live. However, I wish they would not even announce such good numbers...the crazies will just start up again with huge house parties and massive church services! It is only anecdotal, but everywhere I go people are masked and keeping a distance. Please do not kill the momentum! Covid-19 will not abate until we kill it dead!

With no relief checks in sight, evictions are mounting in our area. Thanks for your concern US Senate!

August 27, 2020

DAY 164

A whole new chapter is unfolding in the murdering of blacks by police in America today. The Milwaukee NBA team has boycotted the NBA playoffs over concern for the murder of Jacob Blake in Kenosha, WI. Other major sports teams and individual athletes have spoken out and taken varying forms of protest over this latest episode. It is probably impossible to find a black athlete who has not experience some act of police racism in his/her youth or at least an example of it occurring to family members and friends. Even though an NBA rookie is paid a minimum of $893,000 a season, and most veterans earn in the millions, I do not doubt there is apprehension and fear amongst them if stopped for a traffic incident or an unwarranted search, particularly if they are driving an expensive car. Money and fame do not inoculate or protect them from the hair-triggered hand of a cop. America's gladiatorial entertainment folks have entered society and demand a voice.

Let the games be interrupted!

August 28, 2020

Day 165

Young Mr. Kyle Rittenhouse comes from the same immediate area where my two daughters and seven grandkids live…Gurnee, Greyslake and Antioch, Illinois, the northernmost suburbs of Chicago. Do not want to be too judgmental, but from his earlier photos he is the kid most likely to get his pants pulled down on the first day of school in any year. Reportedly, his mother drove him and his AR-15 across the Wisconsin state line to nearby Kenosha, making him the first terrorist anywhere whose mom escorted him to perform his acts of terror! Spoiled kid…only in America! But, what the hell, if you cannot count on good old ma, who is a boy's best friend, who can a guy count on? Got some dear friends in Kenosha!

Hey, Mr. President, all these bad things that will happen if Biden is elected are occurring on your watch in real time! Seems kind of obvious, does it not? Everything that is going to happen if you lose is really a projection of all your inactions and wrong actions!

August 29, 2020

DAY 166

OK, let us distinguish between "woke" and "wake." Why? Why not? Words and their varying evolutions are fun to know. "Woke" is simply the past tense of the verb "wake." "I woke up in the middle of the night." But it has slid into the vernacular in a unique way. Derived from black usage and later becoming part of mainstream usage, it means to be aware of and concerned about issues of social and racial justice. And, in these times, that is a serious meaning.

As for "wake," a verb and a noun of multiple uses and meanings, context is everything. For example, an Irish gathering to mourn a dead person is a "wake." Apparently, the Irish had a hard time determining who among them was dead. So, family and friends stayed awake and kept watchful eyes for 24 hours after one's "demise." This is where the legend grows a bit sketchy. Usually, a typical family could only afford to lay out the loved one on a bed of ice until a quick requiem mass and burial could be performed. No one could afford a coffin with a lid. But the legend now includes a coffin as a necessity for the story. As a further precaution against premature burial, the deceased Paddy had a bell affixed to his coffin lid, a hole drilled through the lid and a string placed in his hand. If he did "wake," he could signal by yanking the string and be "saved by the bell!"

Stuffed peppers for Joyce tonight!

August 30, 2020

DAY 167

So excited to hear last night that my two daughters and oldest granddaughter will come to Florida in December to celebrate my 80th birthday with Joyce and me. Best gift ever! Only the fives and zeros count. We got together five years ago in Las Vegas for my 75th and it was fabulous!

August 31, 2020

DAY 168

As this month closes, two thoughts. In 14 days, we will have been quarantined six months, one/half year! There are 64 days to the election.

Joe Biden will lose this election if he does not start campaigning with urgency and immediacy. Why is he not in Kenosha, WI mingling with citizens and protesters, meeting the Blake family and the victim, and conferring with the police and community officials about outside agitators coming to town? Mask up, Joe. Walk those streets like Bob Kennedy did in Indianapolis the night MLK was killed. He averted looting and burning by talking to people and sharing their pain and fears. Trump will be there September 1, to ignore vigilantism and Jacob Blake and praise local law enforcement which is akin to Hitler visiting Auschwitz to boost the morale of the furnace crews. Why cede this stage to him?

September 1, 2020

Day 169

I did not know exactly what was occurring at 3:15am today. Our dog, who nightly snores blissfully at the foot of our bed on his blanket, started roaming around as a full Corn Moon appeared in the window. We finally hauled him into bed with us. He went back to sleep while we tossed and turned. And, of course, he was the first up!

He goes by several names and does not answer to any of them. His original name is Casey, but because of his sideways gait he earned the moniker of Uncle Wiggly. During thunder boomers his shivering reactions caused him to be labelled with Neil Young's nom de plume, Bernard Shaky. I just refer to him as my son or the boy. We think he has all the earmarks of a cat, especially his ability to completely ignore us. Yet, he is one mellow dude who never barks or chews or digs. Someone housebroke him perfectly...never an accident! We know nothing about his background except he was dumped in a kill pound and rescued by Senior Paws in Ft. Myers, FL. They said he was seven, but we think he is younger. Still, he is missing nearly all his teeth on the right side of his mouth, but he can gum with the best of them! He seems to lack experience around other dogs, but he is good for a sniff or two. Likewise, cars and trucks and other people get lengthy stares. He is a wonderful addition to our lives...Joyce has proven to be the Dog Earth Mother! I am still trying to master the one-handed reverse bag dog poop pick up maneuver. I have not even tried the twirling effort to tie up the bag's contents. More on that later.

DAY 170

I am going to assume my readers are familiar with the thought experiment that has become the cultural phenomenon known as Schrodinger's Cat. An imaginary live cat is placed in a box and if an imaginary deadly substance in the box decays he will be killed. Thus, as he remains sequestered in the box, sight unseen, he is potentially both alive and dead at the same time. Schrodinger's thought experiment suggests that something can be in two states until it is measured. The necessary measurement would be opening the box and seeing for one's self. To further the interests of science, I have renamed my dog Casey, Sweeney's Dog. The following experiment was tried. When I leave the house by the front door Sweeney's Dog sits and stares out the door's glass waiting for me to return. I left yesterday by the front door, and the dog took his customary position. I quickly returned by the back door via the garage and walked inside to the front door. Said dog turned around looked at me without a note of recognition and went back to his vigil. I then exited through the garage, walked around to the front door where he greeted me happily. I hesitate referencing quantum mechanics too deeply because I do not know what I am talking about. But I am disappointed that my dog did not realize it has been proven experimentally, time and again, that under certain conditions entangled photons and / or electrons can exist in two distinct places at the same time. He just did not get it!

September 3, 2020

DAY 171

Quite a few random thoughts whizzing around in my head. Joyce told me that her nails lady has several teacher clients. The younger ones react well to virtual learning and the older ones hate it. Not surprising for the most obvious reasons. I am beginning to think that the brick and mortar classrooms might be on the way out in the future. There are many glitches in the virtual undertaking...lack of consistent Wi-Fi in the student's home could be a major problem, distribution of texts and accountability in attendance. I have learned the names of several virtual platforms, each having its own strengths and drawbacks. Sometime soon an individual or an educational think tank is going to create a virtual program that fits most needs and is easily applicable to all forms of education.

What about universities and their bloated costs to students? How long can the elite control higher education and force kids into unheard of debt? Are all the students being sent home with Covid-19 getting their tuition and other costs refunded?

What a great chat with my teacher union organizer/negotiator daughter about the state of teaching in the time of plague. One of her superintendents complained about paying building staff when the buildings are empty. She suggested that they be sent to individual homes of kids who are not showing up on the teacher's screen. Sounds like a good plan to remind them that attendance counts!

September 4, 2020

DAY 172

We are back in the stock market. Bought limited shares of Amazon, Tesla, Apple among others as kind of a "legacy" holding. Leave it alone and see what happens. Am anxiously awaiting the Motley Fool's announcement of an "all in buy." Been rumored forever. It may be something 5G related like world-wide Wi-Fi.

Huge profit taking yesterday. But not for us!

September 5, 2020

DAY 173

It is the Labor Day Weekend and I predict a Florida spike in Covid-19 cases. A tourist invasion is predicted. Northerners, pent up for months, get in this Florida party atmosphere and forget common sense. Watch the activity on the Clearwater beaches, Ft. Myers and Miami/Lauderdale closely. Clearwater says we welcome tourist "safely." Yeah, right. That is where the plague started for us at spring break. Back to back, side by side crowds of people on the sidewalks, bars, restaurants and beaches. Merchants begging for business are willing to cut corners and prolong this mess.

ACTUALLY, DON'T COME HERE AT ALL…#notafloridamoron

Just had a long conversation with my old buddy Mel Schmidt in Ft. Myers who is bored to death. Caught up on families and find out that both of us have grandkids who have tested positive. Both were quarantined and now are negative. But who knows what problems might still exist for them?

Got the groceries in and the meals planned for the long weekend. Mussels and ravioli tonight, a proper meal Sunday of grilled lamb chops, peas and little potatoes and Sloppy Joes on Monday.

September 6, 2020

DAY 174

I attended the 1973 American Federation of Teachers Convention in Washington, DC, as a delegate from my Local 1274, Skokie, IL. While searching for an appropriate labor quote for tomorrow, I came across on-line the speech Caesar Chavez made that August 24th day so long ago. He came into the Convention hall escorted by several tough looking guys and under a banner of our Lady of Guadalupe. It was our first look at this diminutive hero who was weak from fasting. He begged us to oppose the Teamsters who tormented the UFA and were in the pockets of the rich growers. This tiny man was near mystical in appearance and speech. He so moved the delegates that one got up and screamed out a resolution that demand a hotel kitchen inspection for boycotted lettuce and grapes! If we found any, we should refuse to pay our bills. Commended by AFT President Al Shanker for its' sincerity, he promptly ruled it out of order!

These were historic times to be in DC. Dinner that night at the Watergate's restaurant. Where we stayed and where the Convention took place was the Shoreham Hotel, the residence of Vice President Spiro Agnew who would resign his office in two months. One year later, Nixon would resign. Ken Drum, Chuck Burdeen and I returned home to call a strike for the first day of school!

September 7, 2020

DAY 175 LABOR DAY

"When a man or a woman, young or old, takes a place on a picket line even for only a day or two, he/she will never be the same again."

Caesar Chavez said this at the same convention. I heard him say it.

September 8, 2020

DAY 176

Our little Casey had an outing this morning. We took him to the dog run at Palm Harbor's John Chestnut Park. It is divided into a fenced area for big dogs and one for little guys under twenty pounds. Those sixty pounders and up ran like crazy chasing each other and anything thrown near them. The short kids engaged in an orgy of smelling everything while following the safety maxim of "walk, don't run." Casey was mesmerized. Several pees and one poop into it, he finally got about eleven feet from the entrance gate…there was that much ground to be methodically covered! He displayed his usual placid demeanor by accommodating all sniffers equally. His tail remained arched all morning, wagging like a metronome. Later, at home, he thanked us for the great time and slept the afternoon away, no doubt cataloguing smells in his dreams.

September 9, 2020

DAY 177

I do not remember why or when we started this but we continued it yesterday. We arranged another string of 200 mini Christmas lights around our outdoor grill and up the wall facing our lanai to replace a burnt-out string. We already have large stalks of sea oats lit up in our living room. We are not Yule decoration fanatics, but these LED lights will burn night and day forever or for as long as we are in this house! Maybe they serve as a signal of welcome to all who see them; maybe they are the protective fire at the opening to our cave. Whatever our original intent, they have evolved into our warmly lit safety shield against the horrific darkness of Covid-19. "Bring light to dark places," the Bible admonishes us and so we do.

Of course, as a literary tribute to F. Scott Fitzgerald, Joyce's fellow Minnesotan, and author of *The Great Gatsby*, arguably the best novel of the 20th century, two green lights burn on the deck continually. Jay never gave up hope, right up to the end.

DAY 178

"Mr. President, there's blood all over your hands, sir!" Not words uttered by any advisor, aide or counselor to him at any point. Under the wild assumption that the President was honestly mistaken in following an avoidance of panic strategy, where were his advisors to tell him he was wrong? They were silent and he chose a route of downplaying and lying for his personal gain while knowing the severity of the coming pandemic. What should have happened was the scheduling of a solemn Sunday evening address to the nation detailing the intelligence reports and the disaster plan left him by his predecessor, introducing his medical advisory staff and setting a date for strict guidelines to be announced. Assurances should have been given that all medical personnel would have unlimited supplies of necessary equipment as soon as possible, manufacturers put on notice for immediate mobilization and, finally, a plea for the full cooperation of our nation. Nothing constructive happened. Obama's plan was thrown out in 2016.

After the 9/11 towers and Pentagon hits, all planes flying in US territory were grounded either in the US or Canada within two hours. Airport security measures were immediately enacted, concentrating on the confiscation of anything resembling a weapon or explosive. Lists of suspects were drawn and, rightly or wrongly, profiling of passengers was put into effect. Quickly, Congress created the TSA under the aegis of Homeland Security. Travelers stood in line after line uncomplainingly. A nation was mobilized and cooperative under clear leadership.

It was totally unlike this present chaotic disaster.

September 11, 2020

DAY 179 (The Twin Towers)

This is the nineteenth anniversary of the attack on the World Trade Center in New York City. The loss of lives of those in the buildings, the loss of lives of the responders, the broken families and the physical damage are well-known facts that will be discussed all day.

In 2012, Jerri Rae and I visited Manhattan. On a tour bus ride up the West Side, I noted a firehouse festooned with flags and red, white and blue bunting. This was the home of Engine 54/Ladder, 4/Battalion 9 located at 782 8th Ave. In that single morning it lost an entire shift, fifteen responders, ranging from rookie Chris Santora to its' captain.

I know an NYC fireman from a different firehouse who traded shifts with another guy for that day. His work mate was killed. He still carries his guilt. My cousin, a Columbus fire fighter, went to NYC and aided in the victim search.

A few days after 9/11, I had to fly to Louisville, KY from Chicago's Midway Airport. The airport was, confusedly, trying to impose some security measures. No one was sure if flights were on or still grounded, but with all the people milling around the area was depressingly silent. Then a group of guys marched through the crowd carrying duffel bags identifying them as Hutchinson, KS firefighters. Hanging from their bags were their axes and haligans. The crowd parted for them and slowly started clapping in unison, cheering and shouting "thank you" much to the embarrassment of these guys. They were on their way to NYC to aid in the recovery! They infused the place with a tiny bit of hope that things might be rectified.

September 12, 2020

Day 180

Golfer John Daly announced he has been diagnosed with bladder cancer. I wish I could sit down with him and discuss his situation. I received such a diagnosis on Valentine's Day in 2012. My internist insisted I see a urologist as an overall health measure. I was 71; Daly is 54. It is not such a stretch to guess where the probe line is inserted to view the bladder surface. After a few moments of viewing, Dr. Richman said: "You have cancer." No sugarcoating by him. The tumor was surgically removed five days later. Treatment, which consists of insertion and viewing, began three months later and continued every three month for three years. Then it moved to twice a year and now once a year. "For how long?" I asked him. "For as long as you are alive," he answered. I am currently cancer free.

By all accounts, mostly his own, John Daly has given up on alcohol rehab. He will find if he drinks any liquid after 9:00pm, he will urinate hourly through an entirely sleepless night, especially if an enlarged prostate exists, too.

Smoking causes this cancer, I was told. I had not touched a cigarette or cigar in 30 years. He is a heavy smoker and probably his damage is already done. He will also need daily medication. A few other complications will arise eventually, but a supportive spouse can help greatly in overcoming them.

I wish him well.

September 13, 2020

DAY 181

It is NFL Sunday! Mike Tirico said: "They made it to the starting line…let us hope they make it to the finish line." Already 16 points up on my pool with the Chiefs' Thursday night win over the Texans. Our pool has 77 members. At the end of today, I rank fourth in points gained. Need wins Monday night. Stories to watch next week: Tom Brady/Bucs comeback and Mitch Trubisky's never ending quest for two good quarters in a row! Many late game cramps and heat exhaustion tolls occurred due to no pre-season games.

My Lord, it was good to have them back! It is probably illusory, but this is the first major sign of normalcy since the pandemic began. Every team has their own version of the pre-game statement. Some kneel, others sit, still others link arms. The Texans simply came out at the kick-off. I think the national anthem is on its' way out, but there are no fans to react yet, except in Kansas City where a call for a moment of silence in support of unity was booed. At least in KC, it is not about the troops, flag or song. It was all a negative reaction to BLM and racial unity. Sad!

September 14, 2020

DAY 182 (We have been in quarantine for six months today.)

I could not help but notice the gap between the President and his audience in Phoenix. Trump was on a dais above and apart from the crowd. Others up there were more than safely distanced from him. Someone tried to approach him, but he cautioned them back. By contrast, his followers were scrunched together in tightly grouped rows of seats or were milling about, arms around each other, posing for pictures while laughing, talking and breathing in close quarters. He who makes a mockery of masks and distancing and testing is tested daily and kept properly isolated while he encourages his cult to mingle in close quarters without a word of caution from him.

September 15, 2020

Day 183 (a continuation)

Though I do not think about Trump's base often, I do wonder why we differ so much?

I watch young, aspiring comedians, detailed by late night hosts, interview his people at rallies. They cleverly trick the unsuspecting into foolish and contradictory positions for a laugh. All this does is make me wonder where and when I diverged from my fellow Americans? Is it their unquestioning religious beliefs? "God sent Trump to us. God will never let me get ill." Or is it their general mistrust of government, i.e. welfare handouts, unchecked immigration, affirmative action, "me too?" There seems to be a growing consensus that, while he promises the moon and seldom delivers, just the fact that he attacks these "problems" seems enough. He speaks to their undefined, inarticulate rage, even against science, and that satisfies them. He is the conman and who to con is his specialty.

Though Trump may be forced from the scene, 40% of Americans remain, unconvinced and defiant, waiting for a Jim Jordan or a Matt Gaetz to step up and fill the gap.

September 16, 2020

DAY 184

I must reiterate…Trump sat on a dais in Phoenix safely above his audience and socially distanced by many feet from the others on the stage. He had tested negative that morning. Everyone on his plane had tested negative. He wore no mask, but no one untested was near him. Someone on the dais approached him off camera, perhaps for an autograph. He stood and emphatically stopped him and backed him off. In short, he practiced perfect avoidance protocol.

If you presented this evidence to his endangered base below, they would have said: "Thank God, he is kept safe," with no regard for their own precarious situation or their own health. This is beyond my comprehension!

September 17, 2020

DAY 185

"Shame at our own dependence on the underpaid labor of others. When someone works for less pay than she can live on---when she goes hungry so you can eat more cheaply and conveniently—then she has made a great sacrifice for you. THE WORKING POOR ARE THE MAJOR PHILANTHROPISTS OF OUR SOCIETY!"

These words were written by Barbra Ehrenreich in 2001 in her book "Nickeled and Dimed." It is important to note that she worked as a waitress and honestly tried to live on her wages and tips. I have much to add to her conclusion in these pandemic times which have fostered the era of "take-out" dining.

Consider this: two people dine out and each has a cocktail and a glass of wine with their entrée. In a reasonably decent restaurant, the bill will come to approximately $100 plus tip, which may be mandated on the bill. Fair enough from an owner who looks out for his servers who, in turn, share with the unseen kitchen workers. However, now for safety reasons you are not dining in, but choosing take-out. Someone preps your food, cooks it, boxes it, bags it up and delivers it to your car. The bill is considerably less. You fail to tip. You eat and drink in the comfort of your home and consider it not a bad deal. WRONG, YOU CHEAPSKATE! The same tipping rules apply to the delivery person, too. Please consider the money you save by taking food out. Tip as if you were eating in!

As for serving those within the restaurant, the wait person now finds new perils, not to mention the constant fear of contagion. Someone comes in without a mask on. He is required to point this out. The patron argues about it but reluctantly puts one on. He will fix this waiter…no tip! The same for the woman who wants a table not properly distanced. "I am the customer!" "Sorry, ma'am." OK, "no tip," she thinks.

Most of us that can afford to dine away from home are not spending money like we used to do. Keep this is mind when your take-out is delivered to you!

September 18, 2020

Day 186

I finished the final book, *The Mirror and The Light*, in Hilary Mantel's trilogy of Thomas Cromwell, preceded by *Wolf Hall* and *Bringing Up the Bodies*, both which I have read. Cromwell was Cardinal Wolsey's aide, a blacksmith's boy from Putney who became a lawyer, and who turned out to be Henry 8th's advisor, enforcer and occasional hitman after surviving Wolsey's abrupt fall from power. We watched the BBC production on Netflix of the first two books and await the final one. This fabulous production, based upon her books, examines a non-nobleman who evolves into a sophisticated and essential operative for the King. And, like any woman who marries Henry or any man who serves him, you can be assured his life, like that of Thomas More, will end badly.

On a slightly less violent scale, I am reminded of the wisdom of one critic who said: "if you work for the Clintons, you had better have cash enough on hand for a great defense lawyer." Serving the great can be a dangerous and costly occupation! I highly recommend reading this Tudor trilogy or at least viewing the Netflix film production.

September 19, 2020

DAY 186

What a bad start to the day! Justice Ruth Bader Ginsburg has died at 87. Bless her, she tried to live until the election. Now the obvious is underway. We had better be at our obstructionist best for the next 47 days. Oh, and we better win the election, or my grandchildren will be saddled with the worst of all courts!

Am out of sorts…eat too much, drink too much, sleep too much, sit too much. Strongly longing for some social interchange, but every time I want to break out, I do not. I am always fearful of catching it. For Joyce and me, no theater, no restaurants, no galleries or museums, no bars or games, no music venues or concerts. I miss crowds and noise and raucous laughter. It will pass…what to cook tonight?

We sent a card and note to Kathy Hite on the passing of her mom. She is the only one from the Hite family who sent a sympathy card to me when Jerri Rae died.

September 20, 2020

DAY 187

A highly informative post on Facebook identifies Ruth Bader Ginsburg as a special kind of Jew. The great Jewish mystic of the Middle Ages, Moses Maimonides, wrote of the eight levels of Tzedakah, which are the varying levels of righteous justice an observant Jew must strive to achieve. It is said that a woman who dies on Rosh Hashanah is a "tzaddeket," or a good and righteous person. However, "Tzedakah" is not simply defined as charity. It is more subtle than that. It means not simply giving things or money, but rather working for justice. For example, giving to a food bank is good, but working toward eradicating the injustice of hunger is an ultimate act, an act that creates a sustainable form of justice. Charity is good but eliminating the need for charity by working for a just world is better. Think of this in the context of our times. We praise billionaires for building hospitals and research centers, but if they were taxed at a rate in proportion to their accumulated wealth perhaps universal healthcare could become a reality for all. A second level of tzedakah is where both giver and receiver of justice are unknown to each other. There is no immediate reward or good feelings felt by the giver and the recipients benefit from an unknown benefactor. Ruth Bader Ginsburg worked for this greater good all her life, having experience from early on the injustices levied on women. It was her consistent striving for justice over a lifetime in everything she did that defined her, not just the day on which she died.

September 21, 2020

Day 188

We are in a pro football pool that includes 77 members. Any fan knows, until the bye days kick in there are sixteen games played over Thursday night, Sunday, Sunday night and Monday night. We pick the winning team in each game and assign a point or points to the team ranging from one to sixteen. As of this moment, The Sweeney family is 15 for 15! Cannot wait for tonight's game… Saints v. Raiders, first game in their new Las Vegas stadium. Never got them all correct before! I will continue this and let you know!

September 22, 2020

Day 189

"Never got them all correct before!" True! Not this time, either. Tied at the half…my Saints went down by ten. Drew Brees never quite as sharp as usual. Gruden did an amazing job keeping the Raiders focused and on task. Got to admit that this season and our pool is so important to our mental health. We have just about run out of options for passing time. Both of us are so sick of politics and these last few days of name calling before the election. Even the death of RBG is not roiling our sensibilities. Bless her for all she did in her generous and wonderful life, but it is not unusual for an 87-year-old cancer victim to die. No matter how vital she is to several movements.

Another dog park day for Casey. He has been asking for one since the last time!

Day 190

Ventured out to dine last night at the Tarpon Tavern for the fish and chips. Best in town and a BOGO on Tuesday nights. The restaurant has an outdoor dining area under an overhang. Two sides are completely open to a breeze. As is the rule, we approached the area from our car with masks on, found a corner table sufficiently spaced and kept our masks on until our drinks arrived. All good. Just about everyone did the same. Except for two old white guys who stood in the entranceway without masks and kept going to a table to pet a security dog. What is with old white guys? I am one but I obey the rules for my own sake first and others later. They were affable and smiling, not gun toting assholes, but why do they think they are exempt? They probably worry about property damage in a protest and are clueless as to trolls infiltrating BLM. Hey, we are old and white and privileged! We do not have to think! I am too but I am learning!

The suffering waitstaff! Because of the freebie dinner more people show up and the servers work twice as hard for smaller bills and even smaller tips. My bill…$32 bucks for three beers and two meals. Tip…twenty dollars and still a deal! Try to make up for some of her losses if you are taking advantage of the specials! You were going to eat there, anyway. They work hard for the money!

Casey enjoyed the park. We sat on a bench and watched him. A man sat on a bench twenty yards away from us watching his dog. Casey sat with him!

September 24, 2020

DAY 191

I know I have an abundance of opinions. That is why I am writing this journal, but usually they do not lapse into my personal self. Yesterday's events which led up to feelings of near devastation will not leave me soon.

I had exactly four tasks to perform. I detached our empty propane grill tank for an exchange. Also, I was going to the ATM, returning books to the library and getting a haircut, in that order. I put the tank in my SUV and thought I had secured it in the rear deck. I got to my bank's ATM to find it was down again. OK, I need to go three miles in the other direction to another Sun Trust bank, but the tank is rolling around and could possibly tear the carpet. I pull into a vacant area to secure the tank in the back seat. When I open the trunk lid it rolls out, bounces a couple of times and gashes my right leg just above my ankle. Blood is running into my shoe, so I go home. Joyce says that it is deep and needs stitches. We go to Urgent Care and get nineteen of them. Back home, we are greeted at the door by a whimpering Casey. I noticed water on the floor and think he had an accident because he missed his mid-morning walk. Joyce said he is wet all over! How could that happen?

We discover the lanai door is open. I had hauled the tank through there and had not closed it. He had fallen in the pool. When we swim, he barely comes near the edge. We have never seen him in the water. There are three semi-circular steps to enter/exit the pool at the handrail. We suspect he fell in there and luckily scrambled from the first step up to the deck. If he had fallen at the deep end he would have never known where the steps are. He would have drowned from fatigue just like my neighbor's little dog did several years ago. Joyce wrapped him in a towel and held him for the longest time.

I could barely look at him. When Joyce went to get Chinese, he came and sat in my lap and, maybe, he had forgiven my carelessness. Maybe I can eventually forgive myself.

September 25, 2020

DAY 192

I just began the newest translation of *Beowulf* by Maria Dahvana Headley. 3,182 alliterative lines written between 975AD and 1025AD by two scribes, designated A and B. As you recall, Grendel, the monster, has terrorized Hrothgar's Mead Hall of knights every evening, killing and eating them. Beowulf arrives in the Danish Kingdom from Sweden to kill Grendel. Brush up on your kennings, meres and scops and wyrds and enjoy this brash, new translation!

In real time I am put in mind, by this legendary epic, of the Republican Senate. As does the monster Grendel, Trump comes to them nightly and, instead of crunching their bones between his teeth, he keeps them physically uniform and moving like humans. But he deleteriously sucks out their souls. Zombie-like, they acquiesce in his scorning of the intelligence community, his trashing of the electoral process, his caging of children, his profiting from his office, his prodigious lying about the plague and all his other affronts to civility and the rule of law. They no longer know us and have given themselves up for dead.

Headley translates at a rapid-fire pace and sets up the macho heroism of men through the ages for a massive fall. Beowulf: "Anyone who fucks with the Geats (a nonexistent tribe from what is now southern Sweden) Bro, they have to fuck with me."

Grendel's mom is her Woman Warrior heroine who wants revenge for her son! Get a copy and read it! Avoid the pain I suffered plodding through the Old English in college!

September 26, 2020

Day 193 (Well over 200,000 victims)

Florida took a giant step backwards yesterday. All bars, restaurants and everything else can be open to full capacity, according to the Governor's sweeping mandate. Things seemed to be going well in our end of the county. A ruling on mask wearing was being observed. You literally cannot get in anywhere without a mask. If this reopening is without conditions state-wide, as the Governor says, how can a local ordinance stand? I was really feeling secure surrounded by masks, but will they now not be a factor? If people are truly afraid as we are, it might prevent them from ever going out. Now everything is open? What if the plague surges as is predicted because of this? Just another set-back for the Trump/DeSantis Florida economy! I sincerely believe that intelligent people will note that nothing is changed by this re-opening. The same idiots who have put Florida in this place will probably go berserk and keep a return to anything like normal forever distant.

September 27, 2020

DAY 194

I just read an interesting article about Warren Buffet's less well-known sister, Doris. She ran philanthropic funds on her own money along with Warren's inestimable cash lode. She read letters from folks with problems. For example, she bought a used trailer for a woman raising three grandchildren, she buried a Mexican laborer and helped scads of single moms, especially those who needed cars. I can almost picture a huge warehouse of serviceable used cars owned by the Buffets. When she did give a car to someone, the title was accompanied by an application for car insurance from Geico, her brother's company. She gave away on average $4800.00 per person accepted. She also managed to give away 200 million of her own money. Never did she contribute to SOBs…symphonies, operas or ballets!

I mentioned earlier that I had a tiny foundation of my own and, like Doris, I never gave to a single charity or religion. I just looked for a person, occasionally a friend, with a temporary need. My favorite encounter was with a young Iraq war vet who was pregnant and in arrears on her rent by three months because of a screw-up by the Veterans Administration on processing her past salaries. She and her little girl were delightful. I paid her rent. If I had Doris' cash, I would do the same things she did as many times as I could, but for now I do what I can!

September 28, 2020

DAY 195

One of our favorite restaurants, Casa Tina, in Dunedin, issued a statement regarding the massive state-wide re-opening. The gist of it was "notwithstanding our Governor's Phase 3 re-opening, we will keep observing the requirements of mask wearing and distancing protocols and rigid cleansing set by the Village of Dunedin. We believe in science over stupidity." If only every place pledged this! To the nuts who want to ignore any establishment's mask sign, do not go there. There are other places that do not care if you live or die. From the pictures online, Florida started on the road to madness yesterday...particularly in Ft. Lauderdale and Key West. Crowds lined up to get into bars, people shoulder to shoulder on the streets, no masks or proper distancing. Joyce and I are never risking our lives for some guy's bottom line!

September 29, 2020

DAY 196

Yesterday I had a cat scan to check on an iliac aneurysm. When I was finished, I went to my doctor's office, said my film was on its' way and made an appointment for Wednesday. The Medical Arts Building elevators are limited to two riders. A woman and I got on. She said to me: "Is this ever going to end?" I said: "What? When we get to our floor!" No, I thought, it is called existence. You must have had a life altering incident or setback sometime, lady. When did your "abnormal" get back to being "normal"? I once received a telegram from my Board of Education ordering me quit a strike or lose my job. I found out my wife had stage 4 cancer on a gorgeous Fall afternoon. I was taken aback by my 17 years- old daughter's pregnancy. I was told I had cancer during a routine check-up. Each situation brought on a "new" normal. These things were not endings, just like Covid-19 is not. They are sign posts on your journey to see if you can navigate a new direction or just wander off, aimlessly. The only thing linear about our lives is our age. All other things zig or zag. They are like the ripples in still water after one throws a handful of pebbles. They lap one another, enjoin each other, expand themselves and eventually disappear. While you live, there will always be new pebbles thrown in your pool.

September 30, 2020

DAY 197

The third quarter ends today. The rest of the world saw last night what America lives with daily.

Donald Trump, made up like a lascivious, aged whore, hurled invectives, insults and lies at the debate moderator, his opponent and the American people. He exhibited all the unhinged madness that is taking our country down along with his pandemic mismanagement and Covid-19 deaths.

His name will not be written here again, apart from announcing his demise or defeat, whichever comes first! (You know I will not be able to keep this grandiose promise, but it sounds cool!)

October 1, 2020

Day 198

I take my dog out every morning at about 7:30 when he wakes up. He is good for three shots or as I like to report to Joyce, a "hat trick." This morning he brought a new wrinkle to the game. After the obligatory three, he walked around a bit, got back on the lawn and took the pose. Nothing came out. I told him four times was just showing off. Henceforth, this shall be known as his "encore."

The efficient lady who trimmed my toenails at the foot clinic today asked me what I did to fill the time. I told her Joyce was studying Spanish and I was writing a book. She was interested in what it was about and how much time I spent on it and when it would be finished. Ms. Carnival told me she has been a reader since third grade, encouraged by her teacher. She asked me a few times if she was hurting me. I assured her she was not. "I do not want to show up in your book looking badly." I told her if everything worked out, she could get it from Amazon and read it on her Kindle.

Ms. Cynthia Carnival, you are in my book!

October 2, 2020

Day 199

He who presides and the First Lady reportedly have tested positive for Covid-19 last night. Hoax? Always a possibility. But this is so far-reaching an assumption and would require coordination impossible to achieve in this administration. Let us wait for a while.

October 3, 2020

DAY 200

What an outburst of creative energy from several people I know! A Crescent Oaks neighbor, Char, just got her first book, *Life's A Trip*, published this week and available on Kindle! My friend and former neighbor Mike Cohen probably is working on the sequel to his last published mystery novel, *Karieth*. Former teaching colleague Samira Ahmed has finished her third young adult novel and Chicagoan Harvey Tillis just sent me his photo book of Jazz, R&B musicians and soul singers taken at Space, a jazz venue in Evanston, IL. just north of Chicago. The book, *Ten Years in Space*, celebrates the venue's decade anniversary. I especially enjoyed the picture of song writer/singer Jimmy Webb who I saw at the Double Door Lounge on Milwaukee Ave years ago. Also, loved his shot of Kermit Ruffin winking at the camera! We heard him play in New Orleans' Bywater neighborhood in 2012.. I talked to Harvey yesterday and we tried to summarize maybe thirty-five years of friendship. He remains one of the kindest, most thoughtful and most interesting persons I know. Harvey photographed my girls at all different ages and took the best family picture ever of Jerri Rae, the girls and me. Harvey's mom once told me that "he is a real mensch." And he is! A copy of his book is on its' way to my friend, John "Nunu" Zomot, a Chicago celebrity photographer.

October 4, 2020

DAY 201

Covid-19 deaths hit 210,534 today. NBC and WSJ polling has Biden with a national lead of 14% over Trump. (Taken since the debate and before the hospitalization.) Biden has smaller leads in most battleground states. Florida tightly holding onto fourth place in new infections. So much for our vaunted DeSantis re-opening of everything. Ironically enough, this massive phase-in well might be scaring intelligent people away from re-opened facilities! Trump's health revelations from doctors and WH remain confused and contradictory. Why does he have as his lead physician an osteopathic doctor rather than an MD? Is it simply because this man gives Trump the answers he likes concerning his weight, his diet and overall strange lifestyle? Dr. Conley needs more clarity and less obfuscation in his pronouncements.

Shrimp and grits tonight. Off to the Tarpon Springs Sponge Docks for just arrived shrimp!

October 5, 2020

DAY 202

I am certain Trump's clown car drive-by caper of yesterday has been chronicled and analyzed world-wide, and there is not much more to say about it. One pundit facetiously remarked: "If you want to know the president's condition, his timeline of infection and treatment, his health status and prognostication, go to the Russian Embassy on Wisconsin Ave NW and talk to them. They know everything." They constantly monitor the cavalier, unsecured activities of the White House. As does Tehran, North Korea and China, I thought. Yesterday, out and about and ignoring quarantine, Trump again neglected his most important duty to us. Just as he has failed us in his lack of concern for Covid-19, he again left us and possibly our allies vulnerable to attack from an enemy power. He disregarded the safety and well-being of Americans. He again failed to protect us.

October 6, 2020

DAY 203

I hesitate turning this journal into a daily political diatribe. There are plenty of papers and social media platforms that handle this sort of thing, but the events of the last twenty-four hours demand acknowledgment. Someone reading this in the future deserves an explanation of the outrageous activities that took place. Trump released himself from Walter Reed Hospital early last night and told America, after 211,000 deaths, not to be afraid of Covid-19. His doctors refused to be forthcoming about any kind of infection timeline for him. He had been filled with steroids and other medicines not yet authorized for general consumption. He returned to the White House, labored up the stairs to a balcony and noticeably and repeatedly gasped for breath. He took off his mask, a gesture of defiance, and entered the Peoples' House as a potential destroyer…an entrance of infamy!

HE IS NOW THE SUPERSPREADER-IN-CHIEF!!!! The White House is Infestation Central! His staff announced there will be no contact tracing of those in attendance at the Rose Garden gathering. If I were to place a bet, a long shot, I would bet he may well be dead within two weeks if he does not honor quarantine. Enough for today.

October 7, 2020

DAY 204

Let us take a break from the madness of King Donald.

Nearing my goal age and, even while crossing my fingers for many more years, I have concluded that hoping for a future beyond my allotted days is not compatible with the essence of my existence. If I have not grasped by now that my very life has been an accumulation of precious days and any more of them to come is an inestimable gift and those will be enough. The greatest lesson I have learned is there is nothing beyond the joy of my existence and any time spent yearning for something beyond is time selfishly wasted. As Camus wrote, amidst the horror, destruction and desolation of Europe in WWII, "We have a duty to be happy." Pay attention to each day!

Reminds me of a joke the little boy tells his dad in the Movie, *The Pursuit of Happyness*. A guy is drowning, and he prays to God to save him. A boat comes by and the captain yells, "we'll save you." The guy responds, "God will save me." He continues struggling and a second boat comes by and the captain yells, "we'll save you." The guy responds again, "God will save me," and then he drowns. When he gets to heaven, he asks God why He did not save him. God replies, "I sent two boats, didn't I?"

Pay attention to what each day tells you!

October 8, 2020

I read a considerable amount. In a year, I probably read dozens of books. I buy quite a few books and now have a library of 1000 volumes. Using my public library card is an ingrained habit from my childhood. Since I taught literature for 37 years, one could say I read for a living. I am a real bitch about lending books. Rarely do it. What do I read? Predominately, fiction...novels and short stories. However, Shakespeare's dramas are a consistent go-to. One strange veer in my reading choices happened recently. I have heard so much about quantum physics or mechanics that I wanted to acquaint myself at least with some terminology. I got a quantum physics for dummies version. And I did learn some definitions and much about Schrodinger's Cat. Also, philosophy, religion and biography have been on my reading plate lately, anything about Buddhism, existentialism and Nietzsche.

The best fiction books I have read in the past five years are:

Ohio by Stephen Markley 2018

The Nix by Nathan Hill 2016

The Goldfinch by Donna Tartt 2014 (forget the movie)

Night. Sleep. Death. The Stars. by Joyce Carol Oates 2020

The Overstory by Richard Powers 2018

I frequently reread in part or whole *The Great Gatsby*, the best novel written in the 20th century, and Ernest Hemingway's short story "Big Two-Hearted River."

I do not own a Kindle.

October 9, 2020

DAY 206

I must include this passage excerpted from a patient's letter to Carl Jung concerning his acceptance of his own nature. Jung felt this was only achievable in the second half of one's life. The parenthetical asides are mine.

"Out of evil much good has come to me. By keeping quiet (for me, by meditating), by repressing nothing, remaining attentive, and by accepting reality—taking things as they are and not as I want them to be—(the perfect definition of Buddhism), by doing all this, unusual knowledge has come to me, and unusual power as well, such as I could never have imagined before. I always thought that when we accepted things they overpowered us in some way or another. This turns out not to be true at all, and it is only by accepting them that one can assume an attitude towards them. So now I attend to play the game of life (I've always said life is a game to be played!), being receptive to whatever comes to me, good and bad, sun and shadow forever alternating, and, in this way, accepting my own nature with its positive and negative sides. Thus everything becomes more alive to me. What a fool I was! How I tried to force everything to go according to the way I thought it out to be! (Could not have said it better!)

October 10, 2020

DAY 207

I have reverted of late to my beloved and delicious Skokie breakfast…a toasted onion bagel, both sides smeared with chive cream cheese and encapsulating generous slices of tomato and purple onion with just a grain or two of sea salt. I go with a Thompson's Bagel since there are no Kaufman's delis or Brooklyn Bagel Boys around. We do have Brooklyn's Lucky Dill on Rt. 19, but it is too far to drive to every morning. What we do have are the most beautiful tomatoes year around with the best vegetables grown here in Central Florida. This is all available at our open-air Farmers Produce Market between us and Tampa! Last night I made vegetable quesadillas topped with salsa or sour cream. Soften up onions, yellow squash, zucchini and red pepper in a little hot olive oil, remove from pan and toast a tortilla. Put the veggies back on the tortilla, add sharp cheddar cheese and top with another tortilla. Flip and toast the top side. Of course, I piled too much on! Difficult flip! Messy but delicious! One of Joyce's favorites and mine, too! Some say Homestead, Florida, at the top of the Keys, is the produce basket of Florida, but I will put my Central Florida growers up against any others! This aging hipster is totally down with farm to table!

October 11, 2020

We are at the pandemic crossroad in our country. The Center for Disease Control, especially through its capitulating leader Dr. Redfield, has been battered by the President to the point of irrelevancy. Our country is torn by Covid-19 and is not coping with it. How can we go forward safely if respected health institutions will not be listened to and acknowledged? Even if Trump's opponent comes up with a sweeping plan of survival, how will Trump's followers accept it after the barrage of criticism and doubt launched against our health experts?

The election itself, barely three weeks away, hangs in the balance. Can it even be properly executed, much less end with a peaceful resolution?

Heavily armed terrorists roam our streets and hatch plots to kidnap elected officials while enjoying the support of a sizeable minority.

To wear or not wear a cloth mask becomes a surrogate for every real or imagined grievance rather than a simple solution to a life and death situation. The death toll scandalously mounts in the United States, and, like the last moments on the Titanic, "the band plays on."

Well, as Brother Malcom said more than fifty years ago: "Chickens come home to roost, y'all!" To this money worshipping, power hungry, reality denying, house of cards of a country that still has not acknowledged its' original sins of indigenous extermination, slavery and systemic racism, they certainly have arrived!

October 12, 2020

DAY 209

I needed a blood test today for my internist. Because my left foot is hurt, I asked Joyce to drive me to the entrance of the Medical Arts Building so I would not have to walk from the parking lot. We took Casey along to wait with Joyce. When finished I called, and she drove up. Since we were changing drivers, we were both out of the car momentarily with both front doors opened. Casey started whimpering and got quite agitated, like he had done one other time. (see August 18 entry) What was it? We were never out of his sight!

He had been wandering the streets of Ft. Myers or Miami, I forget which, when he was picked up as a stray. He ended up in a kill pound. If not for the good folks at Senior Paws Rescue, he would not be here today. They go to pounds and take as many dogs from the kill list as they can handle and put them up for adoption. It occurred to us that he might have been kicked from a car and abandoned. This may account for his fear of car doors opening and humans leaving him.

October 13, 2020

DAY 210

Joe Scarborough said this morning that Trump diehards could care less for the Republican Party, are not sincere conservatives, and have no regard for the roles of senators or cabinet members. For whatever reasons, they worship the President, and nothing will change that, neither logic nor facts, nothing.

I heard a woman on television, without a mask and decked out in full Trump gear, asked if she would wear a mask if Trump said she should. "Of course," she angrily replied, as though the question was patently stupid.

If only...My God! The damage done that could have been avoided!

October 14, 2020

I frequently raise the question with myself as to why am I writing this journal? As it has turned out, and certainly not planned by me, the pandemic and political year have created more than enough to comment upon. Yet beyond this fertile mine of incident and information, the importance of recording one's thoughts, combined with the complexity of how we view ourselves and others, is worth exploring. Let us consider the latter of these two points first.

Psychological studies reaffirm something I think we all know to be innately true. Basically, they conclude that no matter how deep a relationship is between husband and wife or parent and child or any combination of committed lovers and friends, no more than twenty percent of one's time is spent thinking of the beloved. Eighty percent of our thoughts are about ourselves and the things that concern us. In brief, nobody loves me like I love me! With this concept as a given, let us see how it plays out in reality!

(continued tomorrow)

October 15, 2020

Day 212

In his play *Huis Clos* (In Camera, 1944), Jean Paul Sartre concludes that each of us always tries to get the significant other in our life to see us as we see ourselves. In fact, the better our relationship, the more it conforms to our vision of our self. A problem often arises when the other attempts to achieve the same thing. However, accommodations can be made, particularly in marriages, when mutual interest is at stake: financial interests, family responsibilities and social positions. Both parties accept the vision of the other, leave it unchallenged and adjust to it in the most comfortable way. If this is too much of a demand, the relationship usually fails.

Actions, Sartre concludes, are all we have with which to judge each other. Our thoughts can never really determine how we are judged and remembered.

As to the first point, so why write stuff? Quite simple. Maybe someone, in repose, will view our recorded struggles with a more discerning and sympathetic eye then what the mere compilation of our failures, our visible actions, reveal. If actions are all we are to be judged by, then writing is the only possible way of explaining why we took them!

October 16, 2020

DAY 213

I have been re-defined, (according to a friend's recent FB post) not me personally, but me lumped with those like me. I am a privileged, white, cis/het male. CIS means my gender identity is consistent with my birth identity, anatomically speaking, and HET means I am sexually straight. No big mystery here! Got me at white, too. I am that, but "privileged," not so sure. I guess "privileged," meaning automatically included in the white gang world-wide, fits okay, but "privileged" on a personal level, not so sure again. I am saddened for my brothers and sisters of color and have worked with them, marched with them, risked injury with them and mourned with them and have been consistently misunderstood by them until I proved myself otherwise. That is where being white is really a drag if one wishes to relate to others of color on a real level. As for privilege, where was it when I was trying to do three or more things at once just to provide for my family? No regrets, but just being white did not always get me through a difficult day! No racial comparisons are particularly valid, I know. But, just saying, we all live with hardships, privileged or not.

October 17, 2020

DAY 214

Great News: My daughter Caitlen is going to have a baby! Rough guess...early May in 2021! Between Caitlen and Cameron that makes eight grandchildren! Beyond my wildest imagining; Jerri Rae would be beside herself with joy. Boy or girl, it does not matter. Would love a boy, but three years old Julia would want a girl to teach her everything.

Not so Great News: No one is coming to my 80th birthday party, at Joyce and my request. Mike and Jill, Cait, Cam and Jordan plus us are too many folks in one house. We just cannot risk the contagion possibilities. Now that Cait is pregnant, flying should be out of the question. Everyone in agreement, but disappointed. Shoot for 85!

Having Casey the Wonder Dog is like having a little kid around. His toys are strewn all over the house. He never puts anything away! Remember Shari Lewis and her puppet Lamb Chop? Well, Case's favorite is his Lamb Chop doll. The things he does to it makes me turn away in embarrassment!

Talked to my cousin Tom Vincent yesterday. He is suffering from a life-threatening disease and needs constant care. My tiny contribution is calling him and letting him talk about it and its' many ramifications. He never complains about pain or the humiliation of being cared for like a baby. He simply discusses it and recounts treatments. He is an example of a man...no whiner, he! I try to think of him and chastise myself every time I bitch about a tiny pain or inconvenience. How much we depend on our wives! Tom's is a model caregiver. I hope I have the patience to be taken care of and the health to take care of Joyce.

One of us will eventually need the other in ways not previously experienced. Embrace each day!

October 18, 2020

DAY 215

I enjoyed an amazing video today filmed by one of Chicago's premier music chroniclers, my buddy John Nunu Zomot. The Jamiah Rogers Band, featuring Dionte McMusick, vocals and guitar, Aidan Epstein, also on guitar and an unnamed drummer played outdoors at 423 43rd St. on the site of the late and long lamented Checkerboard Lounge. This R & B mecca was located on Chicago's south side in Bronzeville. Started by Buddy Guy and L.C. Truman in 1972, it hosted the likes of Muddy Waters, The Stones, Chuck Berry, Eric Clapton, Robert Plant and many other greats. Buddy Guy left the partnership in 1985. The building, on the verge of collapsing, closed in 2003, but it reopened that same year in upscale Hyde Park at 5201 Harper Court, near Barack Obama's home in Kenwood. Its' doors finally closed in 2015. But today music filled this historic vacant lot much to the delight and reminiscence of a socially distanced crowd!

Dr, Fauci called a "disaster" by Trump...Fauci and other scientists called "idiots," too. Trump lives in the Dark Ages when the world was lit by fire. No electricity, no tech, no health science, no communication...pretty much nothing, just like the inside of his head!

October 19, 2020

DAY 216

Beautiful Saint Petersburg, FL. where the Gulf of Mexico and Tampa Bay meet, lies at the southern tip of my peninsular county, Pinellas. Here Beat writer/icon Jack Kerouac, baptized Jean-Louis Lebris de Kerouac, lived his last years, 1965 to 1969, with his wife Stella and his mother, Gabrielle. The 51st anniversary of his death occurs in two days, October 21st. What brings him back into our local news is the pending sale of his unassuming, one-story home at 5169 10th Ave N. The house has a screened in back room where he wrote and often slept because of the heat. The asking price of $340,000 is way out of line, but the owner is probably hoping for a wealthy collector/fan or literary foundation to buy it. I have seen it and its' décor is 1950's personified. Jack's watering hole was the Flamingo Sports Bar at 1230 9th St. N. He would walk to it. The owner said Jack waited on a bench outside for him to open at 8:00am. His favorite drinks…a shot and a beer. You still can get the Kerouac Special for $2.25. They sell cool Jack T-shirts and once I stopped in to get a couple. My friend and I had a beer and left. We got into my car and looked at each other, "what smells?" We reeked of cigarette smoke! The Flamingo, oblivious to local health laws, is straight out of *The Man with the Golden Arm!*

Jack, an argumentative drunk, suffered a severe beating in 1969 at The Cactus, a segregated all black bar. He died two weeks later at Saint Anthony hospital of cirrhosis of the liver and abdominal bleeding. Thirty units of Type A blood were pumped into him, exhausting the hospital's supply. He was 47.

October 20, 2020

DAY 217

"By sculpture, I understand an art that takes away superfluous material; by painting, one that attains its results by laying on." (Michelangelo)

Where might this provocative quote take us?

October 21, 2020

DAY 218

The art that takes away superfluous material, to lay bare an innate form or idea was the art practiced by Socrates in eliciting a truth from his listener, who knew the truth but could not perceive it until the surrounding rubbish was cut away. It is possible that Michelangelo, who dined at Lorenzo de' Medici's table frequently, may have picked up the idea of the "Socratic Method" of questioning from a passing scholar. Like his contemporary Da Vinci, he had neither the Latin nor Greek to be conversant with such a subject. But he always said that a figure was in the block of marble and wanted to be released. This is borne out by his series of partially emerging individuals with faces that reflect their fierce struggles to be freed. These works can be seen at the Accademia in Florence. His subject was in the marble…Michelangelo said he simply had to cut away and find what was in it!

October 22, 2020

DAY 219

I thought Plato, through artistic arrangement, stacked the deck describing Socrates use of the "method" in the Dialogues. Everyone played their part meticulously. No one ever got tired of Socrates' probing questions. You would think someone got angry at being made to look stupid! But this did not occur with Plato as editor-in control. Valid conclusions were always reached. I could never see how it worked in science or math classes since beginning students really need facts, procedures, rules and laws to tell them how to arrive at any conclusions. It probably works better in a literature or philosophy class where a discussion could be more open-ended. Any good teacher should at least try this technique. However, the danger inherent in these discussions is that students tend to think any opinion rendered is valid. Facts go out the window and arguments ensue. Also, if you probe a teenager too hard, he thinks he is getting picked on.

I found if I could sustain it for fifteen minutes or so, it was a victory. More careful questioning and more cooperative students are needed to take the limitations of the Socratic Method away. We are not all Michelangelo.

October 23, 2020

DAY 220

Obama hit a home run in Philadelphia a couple of nights ago. He attacked Trump on every one of his failings, false promises, inconsistencies and outright lies. One could only imagine 44's sleepless nights the past three and ½ years while dying to scream out in rebuttal. Well, he let it all out and you got the feeling that he could have gone on all night. You could almost hear Michelle saying, "enough, Barack, now stop! You have made your points."

So the debate had no Trump fireworks last night. As one commentator said this morning, "Trump came up one 'lude short. He was subdued most of the night and he paced his lies much better than he did in the first debate. Biden was steady, but low energy. Did some dodging himself, especially about fracking in PA and WV. Upshot, no change, no hearts won over for either side. Biden has never been charged with Ukraine wrongdoing and who cares about Hunter Biden? This situation is frozen in amber like a dead insect until after November 3rd. A debate draw decision for Joe is a win. Trump is demanding that FBI Director Wray go after the alleged Hunter Biden e-mails and that AG Barr start charging everyone in sight. Both could be fired if they do not deliver Trump a knockout October surprise ala James Comey.

And then there is Rudy!!!! What have you gone and done, you crazy old uncle? Who tucks their shirt in while lying flat on their back on a hotel bed? Too many Jeffery Toobin re-runs for you? I am an old, white man and I am sick of crazy old white men! Thanks much, Sasha…NOT!

October 24, 2020

Day 221

We voted yesterday for Joe Biden. Deposited our ballots at our library drop box. Both Joyce and I felt a measure of relief for having it done. Tight race here in Florida and it appears to be a must win state for Trump who, according to the polls, has a rather tortured path to 270 electoral votes as compared to Biden's path. Here is what scares me among the talk of a Blue Landslide! In all the state-wide polls, Trump is always solidly in the forties, percentage wise. These are the people who are proudly for him and have no problem stating it in public. But what about those who keep their votes to themselves? Those folks who are embarrassed to say they want Trump because of family, friends or neighbors' reactions. They are not gun-toting militia people nor do they claim to support Trump's "policies." Maybe they just hate snobbish liberal elitism more than they do Trump's horrible job as President. It does not take much movement for these pockets to put him in play. Joe is certainly beating Hillary's favorability performance and her lack of campaigning strategies. I hope this is enough, but I remain fearful of the unknown.

October 25, 2020

DAY 222

Our dog Casey has been with us 100 days today.

Let us see how this quote holds up to a little scrutiny. It was said by a character named Bishop in Nathan Hill's 2016 novel, *The Nix*:

"Our bodies are the thin knife's edge that separate us from oblivion."

One definition of oblivion suggests "A lack of consciousness." By a lack of consciousness, I think the character means death, synonymously stated as oblivion. Everything that defines us as human beings is contained in our bodies. Our physical faculties, our awareness, our souls, our minds. Even ancient Christianity defines our bodies as Temples of the Holy Spirit, who supposedly infuses us with our souls at baptism. John Donne refences this in his poem "A Valediction: Forbidding Mourning:" "As virtuous men pass mildly away…and whisper to their souls to go…" Only with our flesh and blood bodies intact can we exercise our rational behavior. Only when we breath and when our blood flows and when electrons traverse our synapses can we function on a conscious level. With death, everything goes…our brains, our memories, our stored knowledge, our habits, our abilities, all love, desire, longing, everything. Our bodies that house us, revert to inert matter. Only blind faith in a religious belief, not evidence, contradicts this assessment.

Leonardo Da Vinci dealt with the soul and matter in a slightly different way, but arrived at nearly the same conclusion:

"He saw mind in matter and believed in a spiritual soul but apparently thought that the soul could act only through matter, and only in harmony with invariable laws. He wrote that "the soul can never be corrupted with the corruption of the body," but he added that "death destroys memory as well as life," and "without the body the soul can neither act nor feel." (Taylor, Leonardo, 22)

Remember: Mind is not matter and matter is never mind!

October 26, 2020

DAY 223

(We did go to a restaurant and had dinner indoors Saturday night for the first time. We checked out the social distancing online and they responded with seating pictures on their website. We wore our masks entering and leaving as did the waitstaff all the time.)

Still observing lockdown and avoiding crowds.

Al DuBois Roofing Company is working two doors down from us. The last couple of mornings Al's son Doug, who is the crew chief, shows up just as I am walking Casey at 7:30am. On Monday morning we spoke. He asked me if I had voted yet. I told him we were dropping off our ballots later that morning. He smiled and said: "Trump, Trump, Trump!" I responded: "Biden, Biden, Biden!" We both laughed and disagreed about the last debate. This young Cracker, and I say that not disparagingly because he is pure Central Florida, is not going to offend a potential customer. We wished each other a good day. Today, we resumed the same conversation, but, still skirted around the edges. Talked about Trump walking off the CBS interview. Predictably, we differed as to the merits of Trump's move. He said: "I just hope something gets done after the election." I said: "You know what's cool? We are having a civil conversation!" He laughed and told me my dog was cute!

I have seen Doug around my community. His family roofing company has a lock on this place because of their lower prices. I am certain he is a working guy who probably views much of his world through the eyes of this uncertain economy. Can people continue to afford a new roof? Can I keep my crew together and earning a living? Probably not much else concerns him politically and some liberals usually do not get his problems. He thinks Trump does; he does not, but I know Joe Biden does.

October 27, 2020

DAY 224

I do not know what made me think about this topic since my Catholic elementary school education was useless and seldom recalled. We did learn to read, write, add and subtract, multiply and divide, but it seemed that most of the time we were getting religious axioms drilled into our heads. I know the simplistic rote of the Baltimore Catechism suited a largely illiterate immigrant population in mid-19th century America. But you would think, a hundred years or so later, we could handle something a bit more nuanced. Hey, if it worked for them, it would work on a bunch of impressionable kids. And, for the most part, it did. Adults who have made extremely difficult decisions and career moves, still fall back on these simplistic tropes.

During religion class, which seemed like every class, and assuming Sister was in a good mood and played along with us, we always posed this conundrum: If God is all-knowing, He must know the time of our death. Therefore, all the choices made by our supposed free will only lead us step by step to a predetermined conclusion. Totally ignoring the inevitability of death combined with its' randomness, Sister Mary Something always countered that if we had not made bad choices, we would not have ended up there. This discussion always reminded me of a weary traveler who approached a town with miles to go before home. "If only I had moved here twenty years ago, I would be home now!"

I wish I would have known this joke then. A guy says: "My uncle knew the exact minute, hour, day, month and year of his death." "How?" says another guy. "A judge told him!"

October 28, 2020

DAY 225

Some great quotes that caught my eye recently:

(Chicago Bears!) "Their offense had all the rhythm of a high school reunion dance floor after the open bar had closed," Patrick Finley on ESPN

"Any *norteamericano* who ends up in San Miguel de Allende is either not wanted where he came from or is wanted where he came from." Anonymous

"The Conference of American Bishops could not lead a starving group of vampires to a blood bank." Father Andrew Greeley

As the existentialist said to the non-existentialist: "You have not lived until you think of death every day." Unknown

On her deathbed Alice B. Toklas looked up and asked Gertrude Stein: "What is the answer?" Stein replied: "What is the question?"

Never, ever, under any circumstances, play leapfrog with a unicorn. Jim Sweeney

October 29, 2020

DAY 226

Could not post this on FB…got my second warning. Jail time next!

Jared Kushner, it was revealed, said earlier that a planned neglect of the pandemic was the Trump scheme all along. He announced that Trump had victoriously taken the country "back from the doctors" and "executed" Phase 3, reopening everything. Millions have or will vote for this maniac and the plague will continue, unmitigated by our federal government. Congratulations, young Kushner! You, Daddy in-law, Pence and others have enabled this rolling Holocaust to devastate the country that fought to end the last one! This will be your legacy, this violation of your very heritage! Take a lap, Kush, you earned it!

October 30, 2020

DAY 227

A little political nostalgia and reminiscence concerning the Democrat Party from an aging Dem:

To my knowledge, as a kid trying to understand politics, "understanding" meant understanding the arrangement of the Democrat Party. Every major city had its' own democrat machine. What needed to be known was who was in charge and how firm was his grasp. It was always a given that the Party served the common guy and provided services and jobs. Non-urban Wisconsin was also singled out as an interesting outlier. It brought together farmers and unions in a potent coalition that raised them to a Democrat bulwark status. So the Party became a hard-core, strongly allied constituency of big city politicians, farmers, trade unionists (not public unions), the rare patrician liberal and minorities. How did they lose their stranglehold? Minorities began to demand a bigger share, hence, affirmative action which wrongly appeared to be offensive to many. The rise of the women's rights movement and the consequent denigration of white males and the refusal to acknowledge the complaints, right or wrong, of the middle class all contributed. Finally, a mocking of the religious/social values of the average person by a perceived liberal elite helped finish it off, along with the endless ramifications of the Vietnam War and, lest we forget, the destruction of unions by Ronald Reagan!

October 31, 2020

DAY 228

Borat's latest film is hilarious and worth watching, especially for the Rudy Giuliani clip. Somehow, Sacha Baron Cohen cons him into an interview through his co-star, a young, attractive actress posing as a journalist, in a Westin Hotel suite in Jersey City, NJ. What was this daffy old man thinking, agreeing to this? He arrives early and apparently starts drinking before the "interview" even begins. Was he planning on getting laid? Actually? They commence the interview and it goes nowhere due to her "alleged" nervousness. Rudy assures her with some pats on her knees that she is doing fine. She invites this smarmy old fool into the bedroom for a drink. The best line of all comes when Mayor Rudy asks for her telephone number and address! Is he going to write her a letter? No text #, no Instagram, not even an e-mail request from our hip Rudy…landline# and house address! Too funny! Will not spoil the rest. Enjoy! What is it about goofy, old white guys who think they are attractive? Sorry, lads, give it up! Sean Connery died and you are not his replacement!

November 1. 2020

DAY 229

A new month and two days from the election. The other night we watched the 2017 film, *Wonder Woman*. I read the Vanity Fair feature article on Gal Gadot and wanted to see her perform. She is terrific and the digital action is fabulous. The story is crazy, a total willing suspension of belief is necessary. The WWI Germans become Nazis and the pre-WWII English appeaser, a Neville Chamberlain character, is the universal villain god Ares in disguise. Despite all the mythical re-arrangement, the message of feminine power prevails and the epic conflict of good versus evil comes through. Wonder Woman ultimately finds she needs to fight evil in increments, not just by slaying one dragon. What struck me, by way of contrast, was the way evil presents itself now. Not as the doomed and heroic Miltonic/ Faustian Lucifer of literature who refuses "to bend a knee," but rather as a Donald Trump, who shows us evil as he embodies it… cheap, tawdry, vain and clownish in appearance. He is a vessel of lies, a trickster, a conman and a charlatan. Evil is not a fire breathing Dragon to be vanquished in an epic showdown; evil is Trump, gaudy, tasteless and tacky, but omnipresent in ever shifting forms.

November 2, 2020

DAY 230

What is going to happen tomorrow? Do not know the results, but here is how the procedure was established! We vote for the President of the United States on the first Tuesday following the first Monday of November every four years. If November 1 is on a Tuesday then we vote on the 2nd Tuesday of the month.

Why Tuesdays?

The Founding Fathers determined one could worship on Sunday, ride to the county seat on Monday, vote on Tuesday and be back for Market Day on Wednesday.

Why November?

It is between harvest time and the beginning of bad weather.

If you have not dropped a ballot in a drop box or voted via Pony Express, hitch that mule to your surrey and get your ass to the county seat and vote in person! Time is almost up!

November 3, 2020

Day 231

ELECTION DAY!!!!! More to follow and probably follow and follow ad nauseum and then follow some more!

November 4, 2020

Day 232

No reason to comment as there are eight or so states still counting. Stay tuned! Maybe two days from now.

November 5, 2020

DAY 233

Pennsylvania and Georgia and Arizona still counting. Biden on the cusp at 264 electoral votes. Posted as we learn.

November 6, 2020

DAY 234

Happy tenth birthday to that delightfully sassy granddaughter, Avery.

I believe the stress pressure felt by over half the country, induced by this election, has broken like a fever passing. We have won. It is a matter of finishing the counting in AZ, GA, PA and NV. Most remaining uncounted votes come from Democrat areas. Joe Biden patiently awaits and holds off his announcement. Trump flails, screaming and threatening and lying profusely to little avail. Unrelated and unimaginable grievances are voiced by him and his surrogates. Challenging suits already abound but show little traction. I have no doubt that the international community has turned its' full attention to Biden and what he might do. Trump is malevolent and dangerous, but on his way out. Our national nightmare is still playing itself out. The transformational still wars with the transactional. What remains significant for Biden is maintaining the lead in the popular vote for obvious symbolic purposes. Also, reaching his maximum of 306 electoral votes will have the same unquestioned effect.

November 7, 2020

DAY 235

The isolation necessitated by Covid-19 has been very real for Joyce and me. We have not suffered materially and our relationship has deepened, but health issues and our ages compel us to rigorously follow proper protocols. We miss our families and our freedom. Everyone probably feels this. What has worn us down is the continual stupidity of our president and his cult-like following. The selfishness of many in refusing to combat this plague is incomprehensible. The very people who avoided science and math courses dare to question doctors who have honed their expertise on years of study and experience. How did we become this way? What makes certain people so inherently dumb, so unquestioning and so gullible? As an observer of teenagers for thirty-seven years, I relate the adults to their pasts. Those who cannot write two coherent grammatical sentences in a public forum comment are the same teenage non-reading blockheads who reveled in their ignorance. It is a cruel but accurate assessment and it has nothing to do with our educational system. No system, however flawed, teaches ignorance as an objective.

November 8, 2020

DAY 236 PENNSYLVANIA PUTS JOE OVER!!!!!!

Joyce and I watched the joyous victory lap of Joe and Kamala last night. She said: "Don't you wish we could be there?" I said: "No," it's a night for the young. My street dancing days are over." But seeing young people all over the country celebrating raised our spirits greatly.

Joe and Kamala and Pennsylvania, at least partially, lanced the national carbuncle and provided a modicum of relief to the faithful. Most importantly, Kamala Harris brought women, especially women of color, to a newly raised platform. Acknowledgement is finally being paid to black women who have held together a race while nursing us whites and raising us and cleaning up our messes for centuries. She is magnificent and she emphasized the black voter contributions to this victory. Rep. Jim Clyburn and South Carolina blacks put Joe on the road to the nomination and Stacey Abrams carried them over the finish line in Georgia and may yet give them the Senate, too!

In a complete physical rebuke of that loathsome oaf, Trump, Joe Biden sprinted down a ramp and gave a full throated, gaff-free repudiation of the last four years. A bit too heavy on unity and forgiveness for me and many others, but that will be discussed later. Last night felt good.

After November 3rd, when the election hung in the balance, Joyce and I came as close as ever to a hint of despair. How can we handle four more years? We cannot go anywhere. No place wants us. Even our lovely home was closing in. We had nowhere to retreat except further within ourselves and that was not a healthy alternative. Then, bit by bit, the red mirage lifted and we are in a better place that will only get better!

November 9, 2020

DAY 237

I'll bet anyone passing the toll way exit in Philadelphia to The Four Seasons Landscaping Company will now and forever recall the most bizarre press conference held there! I hear the name and Vivaldi goes off in my head! This company is not part of the Four Seasons posh hotel chain, even though they are inextricably linked in the Philly area by Google, the yellow pages and various phone books. Who made the initial mix up is unknown. The owner said he was called by the Trump campaign to hold a press conference because he had plenty of space. (yep, in front of his garage) "Hey, for the free pub it was fine by me," he said. And so the location was secured, flanked as it was by a porn shop featuring rare, out of print soft core photos of "Be Best" Melania and a crematorium emphasizing Don's role in the thousands and thousands of Covid-19 deaths. Front and center was America's inimitable Clown Mayor, Rudy (I was tucking in my shirt!) Giuliani, gesticulating wildly all the while with both hands free, for a change! Well on his way to a certifiably disordered mental status, the bug eyed Rudy rolled out the erstwhile voter challenging suits against at least four uncounted states and incoherently tried to explain whatever it was he was trying to explain! Not even Eric's muddled appearance could top this scene! The presser ended chaotically, and the owner of Four Seasons currently is "raking" it in selling "law(n) and order" T-shirts!

November 10, 2020

DAY 238

Today would have been my mother's birthday. She was born in 1907 and died in February of 2009 in her 102nd year. If she had been born a Himalayan, she would be 112 years old today. Just "getting up there in years" by Tibetan standards! She was a mercurial force in my life and every shift in her mien demanded wary attention. I have often thought that she was born in a time too early for her desires. She was as bright as could be and earned a scholarship to a pricey Catholic academy at a time when not every girl went to high school. She and her sister had good jobs in Columbus' financial district which kept their family afloat in the Great Depression. This independence haunted her for the rest of her life. Marriage and family and the times stymied any of todays' outlets for her. She poured herself into volunteerism and being a good corporate wife and mother, but I do not think this was enough. I posted a picture of her on Facebook this past Mother's Day. She was probably nineteen or twenty at the time with a beautiful head of dark hair, fashionably slim and an enigmatic look on her face. She was a Fitzgerald girl with a secret or two. She may well have added others over the years.

November 11, 2020

DAY 239

Trump fired the Secretary of Defense days ago. No great loss. Today three key people under him fired; all four replaced by hacks. We are at a security risk with this lame duck madman. The FBI and CIA directors are next to go. All the replacements now have two months jobs. Joe Biden blocked? NOT! I cannot believe that the President-elect, through his transition team, all experienced Washington insiders, will not have access to all information available by a variety of routes. Recount in Georgia…nothing will change.

French toast and our new favorite Chicken Italian sausage stuffed with spinach for dinner last night, A possible tornado with cocktails tonight. A culinary surprise for Joyce tomorrow night!

Forget the tornado, ETA is coming through with big winds, tons of rain and flickering lights!

November 12, 2020

DAY 240

Normally I avoid numbers when writing about Covid-19 because they change so rapidly. But here is a snapshot of today...10.5 million cases, and 242,000 deaths in the USA. How intertwined is the plague and the economy? Almost totally! We are in a second wave that is seemingly bigger than the first or, as some experts put it, in a huge surge of the first wave. Think for a moment and set aside the personal loss of each death and just imagine what percentage of wage earners was removed from the economy. Probably thousands upon thousands. Then consider the 10.5m cases. Exclude youngsters and seniors and think in terms of recoveries and quarantines. An almost incalculable number of workdays lost, that is, wages and production. The problems piggyback endless upon each other. One elementary class exposed and quarantined eliminates one teacher and maybe thirty parents from work to supervise the required quarantine/recovery time for their child. Only masks and distancing can slow this monster down. Re-opening more and more of society and pretending that normal activity will do the trick is a fool's game. Nothing has replaced the proven protocols. Concentrate on them and economic results will follow. But not until...

November (Friday) 13, 2020

DAY 241

Not your day, Parakavedekatriaphobes! Do not get smug, Friggatriskaidekaphobes! You are in the same boat. Check them out, reader! #13 disasters...the Last Supper, Tupac's last day, friends and/or enemies of Jason the slasher and any guests with a room on floor 12a in any hotel. Half the hotels in Vegas have a 13th floor so do not push your luck there!

November 14, 2020

Two spiritual and philosophical heroes of mine are Thomas Merton, the Trappist monk and author and Albert Camus, the French author. I saw Merton sixty years ago (Spring of 1960) at his monastery, the Abbey of Gethsemani, in Kentucky. I was in a choir loft seat during a retreat and he was pointed out to me as he exited the main floor of the Abbey church. His cowl covered his tonsured head so I could not see his face. Merton died in Bangkok eight years later. There is an amazing life-size sculpture of him on the campus of Bellarmine University in Louisville, KY. As you approach it, he almost leaps out to embrace you with an impish grin on his face. Both men, born within two years of each other, died in the turbulent Sixties. Merton died by accidental electrocution in Bangkok in 1968 and Camus in a car wreck after leaving Lyon, France in 1960, the same Spring I saw Merton at Gethsemani. Merton acknowledged people like Camus and Sartre when he wrote: "an atheistic existentialist has my respect: he accepts his honest despair with stoic dignity. And despair gives his thought a genuine content, because it expresses an experience---his confrontation with emptiness." To my beloved monk--"Thank you, Frater!"

November 15, 2020

DAY 243

Existence and Essence

Some theologians and thinkers have posited the notion that our essence is of primary importance. Socrates thought that all knowledge that we acquire was merely a recollection of what we knew before we existed. Catholicism and most Protestant religions define us as being created in "the image and likeness of God." Judaism suggests that we are children of Abraham. Even the Romantic poet Wordsworth in his *Ode: Intimations of Immortality* suggests that our souls at birth are… "trailing clouds of glory do we come/From God, who is our home."

What is wrong with this identification of our essences is that it leaves us little to do by way of developing and defining ourselves. How many of us, educated in parochial schools, still fall back on a rote spiritual definition of oneself learned at the age of six! "Who made me?" "God made me to know Him, to love Him and to serve Him." This indoctrination, combined with familial and societal pressures, can lead to an automatic, even robotic, spiritual life. (continued)

November 16, 2020

DAY 244

Let me pause the ongoing discussion. Between November 25, 2020 (the Thanksgiving travel day) and January 1, 2021, we will experience possibly the most dangerous period any of us have lived through, if we live. Do not travel... do not gather indoors...avoid crowds...wear a mask when you should!

Bear with me as I continue. It is my belief that existence must take precedence over essence. I cannot be anything unless "I am." Only then, and assuming the task starts when I have attained some use of reason and some independence of thought, can I define my essence or "who I am." This is a lifelong process and it must not result in only being identified and imprisoned by my occupation and avocations. This can be catastrophic if one loses his job, if that is his total identification of self. Particularly in American where income and status rule, this often happens with disastrous results. I cannot stop the pressures to define me by my family, peers and society, but at some point I must rely upon my own feelings, experiences, intellect and beliefs. I must not fall victim to an essence defined for me and imposed upon me, whether spiritual or secular. This is a good reflection and reminder to one even in his 80th year!

November 17, 2020

DAY 245

So, I exist and I have a good handle on what I have become. Then someone comes along and tells me my existence and my condition is 'absurd.' I guess now I am in a state of ennui and nothing really matters. Like Svidrigailov in *Crime and Punishment*, I will lead a life of cynical hedonism and then commit suicide. No, it is not that kind of absurd, and it is not absurd meaning silly, foolish or boring. My state of absurd is 'nonsensical.' It makes no sense.

What is absurd about our human condition is that only we, alone in the known universe, residing with animals, plants and minerals and a lot of subatomic stuff, possess the intellect, the curiosity and the rational tools needed to ask a variety of questions on the same theme. "Who am I?" "Where did I come from?" "Where am I going after this life?" The very fact that we belong to a species that can even formulate such questions is amazing. But cruelly, there are no answers or responses from a cold and silent universe. How can we have faith in the unseen and hope in the unspoken? How do we deal with this cosmic joke? Only by accepting responsibility for all our actions and only by the love (caritas) and service to those around us can the worth of our lives be determined.

November 18, 2020

DAY 246

My namesake grandson, James Armando de la Paz age fourteen has a mighty flair for the dramatic and a ground level tolerance for pain! Turns out James was practicing football with some of his buddies on their own; he took a fall and broke his collarbone. Yesterday, he had surgery to put in a plate and screw. When he woke up in the recovery room the nurse asked him how he felt. James announced that the pain was "terrible." The nurse said: "That is interesting considering you are still sedated!"

Senator Chuck Grassley (R-IA) caught my attention this morning. Grassley, the oldest US senator at eighty seven years, has Covid-19. He announced his family will forgo their usual large Thanksgiving dinner. He said his wife and he are quarantining, wearing masks and observing social distancing, as if this will hasten their recovery. Sorry, Senator, that is what you should have done. They are preventive measures, not cures! Grassley reportedly never wore a mask before. Best wishes, sir!

November 19, 2020

DAY 247

We saw an interesting outdoor production from our car at the always creative freeFall Theater last night. Four singers on a plexiglass separated stage recreated the Orson Wells, Mercury Theater, radio program "War of the Worlds" complete with jumbotrons. Calling it a love letter to Tampa Bay, the show included a local newscaster breaking in with increasingly frantic alien invasion announcements. Plant City, the Strawberry Capitol of the world, was targeted and ultimately vaporized, along with an on the scene reporter. A friend once told me that Plant Citians thought "Talladega Nights" was a documentary! The Kanye West administration seemed helpless in the face of this attack! We all applauded the singers' upbeat songs by honking our car horns, just like a Joe Biden rally. Eventually, the invaders made us promise to love them and one another. Talented local drag queen, Matthew McGee, played every alien part! Finally, Mayor Rick Kriseman of St. Pete brought the show to a close with a heartfelt cameo message of "can't we all just get along?"

A minor aside…my old friend Mel Schmidt called yesterday from Ft. Myers. He asked if I would get the vaccine. I said, "sure." When he found out I would be 80 in two weeks, he suggested, facetiously I hope, that it might be a waste of a dose! Mel is three years younger and he feels that, unlike me, he has a lot to live for! LOL!

November 20, 2020

DAY 248

It was my honor and pleasure to teach Advanced Placement English students my last eight years. They were gifted, highly motivated kids happily given to speculation about themselves. Prior to graduation each year, I discussed with them their futures and their choices. Bright as they were, they readily assumed the whole world was open to them. Everyone told them so. "The skies the limit!" "Write your own ticket!" "You can become anything you desire!" I merely suggested they turn around their telescopes into the future and view it through the large, narrowing end! We had read Frost's poem "The Road Not Taken" and, like many, they enjoyed the seemingly bucolic ramblings of this innocuous old timer. "I took the one less traveled by,/ And that has made all the difference. "Is it a good or bad difference for him? Do not assume anything he says or does not say. Choices, decisions, possibilities, random happenings in Frost's hands are time bombs, not necessarily set to detonate immediately. Choices narrow and limit everything. You can sample and sample but at some point something or someone makes you choose. Where I go to college and what I choose to study limits me. I might not know my occupation, but It is highly unlikely I can be both a surgeon and an astronaut! If I have not met my future husband or wife at college, I well might in the town where I work. And this will further limit where I live. For most folks marriage limits their exploration in that field of choice. In fact, marriage and work often jointly determine and limit most options. Say I work and live in Chicago and love it, but my company's headquarters is in Decatur, IL. If I want to advance, I may end up there. There goes Chicago and Malibu, Key West and Cape Cod! My wife wants to live near her mother who is a disabled widow. How can I say no? School, work, marriage, children, homes, mortgages and other unforeseen responsibilities narrow, narrow and narrow our choices. Options shrink with each passing year based on one's commitments.

A friend of my parents told me the night of my high school graduation that "the best years of your life are behind you." No need to despair! They were not behind me! Not a single thing I planned for, if I even did, turned out…but all that did happen was so much better!

November 21, 2020

DAY 249

If you are still considering choices and their inevitability, check out the irony in this Middle Eastern Tale that is over 1000 years old.

A master sent his beloved servant to the marketplace on an errand. The servant hurriedly returned quite agitated. "What's wrong?" his master asked. "I saw Death at the market, and she gave me a bleak and deadly look that terribly frightened me! If you would give me a fast horse I can be in Samarra by evening and be away from her and my probable fate!" The master loved this good and faithful servant so he saddled his best horse, gave him some money and sent him on his way. Later, he got to thinking about this incident and grew angrier and angrier at Death. He went to the marketplace, sought out Death, and said to her: "Why did you scare my servant out of his wits?" "That certainly was not my intent," replied Death, I gave him a look of surprise and astonishment at seeing him here because I have an appointment with him tonight in Samarra!

A bit surprised that Death is a woman! Not going to touch that one! This tale was first used in modern times by British novelist Somerset Maugham and later adapted by John O'Hara in his 1934 novel *Appointment in Samarra.*

November 22, 2020

DAY 250

On Friday, 11/19, 2020, Florida Governor DeSantis announced the five Florida hospitals prepared to receive and store and administer the first shipments of the vaccines pending FDA approval potentially within three to six weeks. Broward and Dade, Jacksonville, Orlando and Tampa General hospitals have been tapped. All have the cold storage capacity for the Pfizer product.

Five million syringes, needles and swabs have been purchased by the state. Another vaccine which does not require unusual refrigeration can be issued by CVS and Walgreens. No sign-up or orderly inoculation process has been announced. First responders and long term care facilities will get obvious priority ranking. Recent therapeutic medicines have become available, too.

I wonder if any of this rush news has anything to do with a certain guy who takes up residence in the Sunshine State on January 21, 2021?

November 23, 2020

DAY 250

Today, 57 years ago, John Fitzgerald Kennedy was assassinated in Dallas Texas. I was in the Christian Brothers Monastery in Glencoe, Missouri. Late in the afternoon we were told he had been shot at approximately 12:30pm and that he died about 30 minutes later. That was all. We went into total silent prayer mode. Details were available to us novices on Thanksgiving Day, six days later, when we got permission to read newspapers and magazines.

November 24, 2020

DAY 251

Rudy's son has Covid-19 so Rudy is supposedly quarantined for being "exposed." If you are aware of Mr. Sasha Cohen's latest film you will love the delicious irony abounding in that word! Also, Florida Senator Rick Scott and little Don Jr. declared "officially diseased." Of course, poor Eric is left out again! Today, Melania sent out the much sought invitations to the White House Holiday Party on November 30. Poe's "Masque of the Red Death" is the adopted theme. Come for the festivities; stay for the plague! Do not miss this once in a lifetime gathering!

The GSA released transition money, access and space to elected President Joe Biden. Certification in Michigan finalizes vote guarantees in every disputed state.

Rudy's legal gang is down the tubes for good. When Trump is embarrassed that is as bad as it gets! One victory in thirty-four lawsuits just did not cut it. Hey, they did succeed in getting Republican vote observers six feet closer! As mentioned, Rudy G. is conveniently out of sight as his disbarment proceedings are filed with the bar association by a New Jersey Congressman.

November 25, 2020

DAY 252

Here are some facts: exit polls show that Trump won the white non-college vote over Biden by a 68% to 31% margin. Trump got over 70 million votes, presumably from Republicans. Approximately, 2.8 million black folks voted for him, with marginally educated white people providing the overwhelming majority. Black people tend not to buy any conspiracy theories except one (which is a reality, not a theory). For over 400 years they believed that white people discriminated, deprived, denigrated and denied them routinely and who can disagree? Thirty-five million white republicans think the election was rigged. I am not sure how this was accomplished and why was I left out? It must have taken a ton of planning to get rigged machines into hundreds of counties in AZ, PA, NV, WI, GA and MI, not to mention buying off all those republican vote counters and elected republican officials. How shabby was the rigging to overlook Mitch McConnell? Not even George Soros and the Koch brothers money combined could afford such an undertaking. Also, consider the difficulty getting the same persons' attention off that nationwide pedophile ring run by Hillary Clinton from a District of Columbia pizza parlor to concentrate on this caper? Religious upbringing fits in somehow. If you were taught from an early age that a young middle eastern virgin was impregnated by a bird and you still cling to talking snakes, resurrections, reappearances and ascensions, then, just maybe, you are a candidate for conspiracy theories and Trump promises. By no means do I leave out Evangelicals. You speakers in tongues and rapture holdouts are in this mix, too. Someone smarter than me has got to link, statistically or at least anecdotally, uneducated whites who hold childish notions with current religious fanatics who believe any crazily cobbled explanations for the ills of the world. Or are you all the same people? The divide in this country is between those possessing a historical and philosophical perspective and those who do not. And that requires higher education and lifelong learning. If you do not possess the will to achieve this then, at least, use some common sense!

Joe Biden is still the elected President. The other guy is not! Sorry.

November 26, 2020

DAY 252

I do not doubt that airline terminals are bustling today with thousands of people ignoring the stay at home guideline. I believe, as far as Covid-19 guidelines are concerned, that this country is ungovernable. Maybe it is that, unlike many countries, we have never lived under an authoritarian regime. Maybe we were never "broken in" as far as mass compliance goes. If we had lived in London during the bombing raids, we would have left our lights on! We have been contrarians from the beginning. We simply do not comply as a nation unless stringent punishment is attached. As far as most laws are concerned, we obey because it is in our own selfish best interests. I generally avoid running red lights because I could get killed. I do not kill people because their relatives might kill me. I do not own a gun since there are so many fellow citizens I would like to shoot. And on and on.

Joe Biden is right in not shutting this country down again or even mandating masking laws. The situation has gone way beyond these restrictions. If one is not moved by humane concerns for their fellow citizens, nothing much else will move them, even their own health and the loss of loved ones. All he and we have left is the vaccine. Get it approved and get it distributed as soon as possible. Take the shots and continue to isolate yourselves from the anti-vaccine kooks. Latest polling shows 42% of Americans not interested in a shot! Protect yourself the best you can. The contrarians will always inhabit American soil!

I am taking Thanksgiving off. I am not giving thanks for anything. I am glad I have my wife. I am glad I have her family and my family, our children and grandchildren. I am glad to have my friends who I love like family. I am glad Casey is with us. I am glad for a comfortable life and a beautiful home. I am glad to have decent health and insurance for both of us. I do not thank anyone for any of these people and things I mentioned. No one, no unseen power, gave these to me. No thanks are necessary. No explanations needed. My life could have gone one way or another. This is the way it has gone.

November 27, 2020

DAY 253

On this day consider the injustices visited upon Native Americans from the very beginning of our presence on this continent.

I am glad that we have front line workers, teachers, essential workers, scientists, poll workers and everyone who voted for Biden.

November 28, 2020

DAY 254

I love the day after Thanksgiving! Still a lot of good things left to eat and we bring the trees and decorations in from the garage. We turned our living room into our reading and music listening area some time ago. A table stacked with books and magazines separates our chairs. If we reverse our recliners, we can view our pool and lanai area and the pond beyond through two sliding glass doors. Just past the doors will be our first tree. The second will stand in a corner of the great room. The outside one is mine to decorate. My old man was a Christmas tree artist! No one dared touch a thing. He arranged the lights and each ornament.

We all sat and watched as he finally finished draping each individual icicle. I am as obsessed as he. Joyce has her tree; I have mine!

I just got 600 LEDS from Amazon Prime! Once strategically placed, my lanai lights will probably divert commercial air travel!

It is up and decorated with 300 extra lights! Looks great! OK, I cannot resist! Guy buys a Christmas tree from the tree man who asks: "Going to put that tree up yourself?" "Nope, going to put it up in the living room!"

November 29, 2020

DAY 255

I was saddened to see a picture on FB of my cousin Joan's family taken in their garage as they exchanged Thanksgiving dishes. Vietnam vet Marine John Keir, Joan's husband, is now in a scooter. He suffers from the effects of Agent Orange. This robust science teacher, coach and fanatic golfer has paid the price for his country tenfold. A "Thank You for Your Service" does not go nearly far enough!

Joyce's tree goes up today along with stockings at the fireplace and wreaths outside. I got Casey his Christmas stocking at CVS yesterday, red with a white C, hung in the middle right under the mantle. How much fun is this guy!

Meatloaf, mashed potatoes, gravy and peas tonight.

November 30, 2020

DAY 256

Florida logged its' one millionth Covid-19 case yesterday. In another day we will surpass this record. This month has gone on forever. Joyce and I are feeling fatigued after rushing around and decorating the house like Christmas means something this year. Our fatigue is really Covid-19 related; what we and probably anyone with half a brain suffers from. We protect ourselves, avoid any danger and do not even comment on the stupidity of others.

I am turning my attention fully to tomorrow…our second anniversary! Now just thinking about that makes me happy. Got the card and the gift ready and dinner is planned Also, am having a desk/worktable made for Joyce's office of that fabulous Costa Rican "parota" wood. Stopped by Tampa Bay Salvage this weekend. The fabricating of the table goes on and it should be delivered this coming week!

Two years of marriage, four years and three months together, and we never run out of talk or stop making each other laugh.

A phone call got us up at 6:03AM. Pinellas County Emergency Weather Service warned of a possible tornado in our area of north county. We find from TV weather we are just outside of the boxed tornado area. Winter in Florida!

December 1, 2020

DAY 257

It is our second anniversary today! We have been together over four years. I bought Joyce an upgraded Fitbit; she gave me a subscription to the New Yorker. We will work out today, take the dog for a walk and then champagne and a rib eye for dinner. We often talked about our lockdown and what an abrupt ending it brought to attending college and pro games, fishing in the Keys, concerts and theater, planning travel and enjoying Tampa Bay's huge selection of restaurants. We certainly did not conclude it was a great thing to miss so much of our families and friends lives, but quarantine surely quickened our senses of introspection/ reflection on where our lives have been and what they may become. Time is not on our side and at our ages our health can turn on a dime. We have read and studied and discussed so many topics. We have watched and appreciated so many missed films, listened to so much music and read so many books. We have reveled in the defeat of Trump and come to love Joe and Jill. Most of the craziness of our years has passed: the struggles, the competitions, the gains, the losses. Consider us at peace, temporarily.

December 2, 2020

DAY 258

In 2018, Joyce and I lived the month of August in Florence, Italy. Both of us had been there before, but we spent considerable time reading and studying this Cradle of the Renaissance and its' geniuses. I read Walter Isaacson's biography of Leonardo Da Vinci. Leonardo, born in 1452, kept notes from 1480 until his death in 1519. In 2002, I also spent a month in San Miguel de Allende in Mexico and wrote a journal style account of the last days of beat icon Neal Cassady who died there in 1968. It was published in an e-magazine called "Mex Connect" in 2006 and is still available on-line. My point in mentioning this is to explain the "journal" method of writing that I engaged in there and here. I am comfortable in this writing mode. Da Vinci's ongoing record provides a massive amount of detail on the thoughts and observations, random and/or profound, of this giant. More than 7200 pages exist over 500 years later, and scholars assume this to be only a quarter of what he wrote!

December 3, 2020

DAY 259

The above pages referenced are a larger body of information than all the digital documents and e-mails Steve Jobs accumulated throughout the 1990s. These papers have been packaged in various codices or handwritten pages bundled together. Bill Gates owns one such codex. They are not numbered nor organized by topic. If you viewed a transcript of any one page you would be baffled by the sheer number of references, details, questions to be asked and sketches. Why such a hodgepodge? Writing paper was extremely expensive and Leonardo used every inch of a sheet recording related and non-related items.

December 4, 2020

Day 260

Was Da Vinci a genius? Of, course, he was! He saw the universal relationship between the flow of blood in the human body from the aorta through its veins and capillaries to its extremities, and all waters forcing their way via creeks, rivers, and channels to the sea and plants and trees pumping nutrition to their branches and fruits. This was a man who could not learn Latin and did not read a book until they were printed in the Italian vernacular. He accomplished everything by observing, sketching and recording. He imagined the unimaginable. He dissected corpses to understand the body's mechanics and make his art as perfect as possible. He analyzed the rise and fall of waves by the effect of wind "upon the amber waves of grain." The grain bends and leans, but never moves nor do the waves! He correctly designed but never carried out the flying machine based on his study of birds; he created the prototype of SCUBA gear; he sketched in detail endless military vehicles and weapons, and he invented and perfected cranks, gears and pully systems. He applied to the Duke of Milan's court with the first "resume" ever written listing his engineering ideas. The last line is forever noted in history:

"Likewise in painting, I can do everything possible, as well as any other man, whosoever he may be!"

December 5, 2020

DAY 261

Some critics suggest that modern art began with *The Last Supper*. It is a freeze frame produced after a camera has rolled left to right recording the varying interactions of his groupings while the main subject remains immobile in the center.

I agree with author Walter Isaacson that the late Steve Jobs was our Leonardo Da Vinci. We live in his world daily.

December 6, 2020

DAY 262

A wonderful birthday present arrived yesterday from the kids…a new chair for my office. "Old faithful" and the pillow I have graced are on their way out as soon as I can get someone to assemble the new one. Bought Joyce a new one yesterday to go with her new worktable.

Advice to myself:

I am drawing down to the end of my project. Like any writer, I wonder if anyone will bother reading this? I suppose all old men think their lives were unique and the wisdom they share is invaluable. I probably thought this some-time, but I was wrong. The best I can do is not make a fool of myself on paper or in person. Keep a degree of dignity and do not venture into areas where I know nothing. Avoid avuncularity. That is even worse than stupidity. Listen to younger persons' explanations and learn something. Ask questions and do not be afraid to expose myself to something new. Keep informed. Know facts. Do not rely on past information that may be obsolete. Do not rely on assumptions. They are generally wrong. I cannot believe everything my wife tells me. Of course she will say I am cute! Remember, she is building her own resume, too! I will respect my adult children and hope they know what they are doing. I do not have to be my grandchildren's pal but I will give them whatever they need. I enjoy my friends and will not be too judgmental. They are not any goofier than me. I cherish my wife. She is all I will have in the homestretch.

December 7, 2020

DAY 263

The attack upon Pearl Harbor's American military installations by the Japanese Empire occurred 79 years ago today. We sustained 2,403 American casualties. In the recent past, we have equaled and exceeded that number by way of daily Covid-19 deaths. What Japan did to us pales next to what our failed leadership and our personal stupidity has done.

I was born on December 9, 1940. An internal problem was detected in me almost immediately and a high risk operation was necessary. I was baptized and survived the procedure. The following December my family celebrated my first birthday in Columbus, Ohio with our relatives. It was a Sunday, two days before my actual birthday. Maybe a radio was on for some background music, but somehow news came of the attack. I can almost imagine my mother's words: "Pack the car, Bill, we have to get home." I am sure their fear was palpable and they prayed a rosary for the dead and injured on that ride into a precarious future.

December 8, 2020

DAY 264

Today is the Feast of the Immaculate Conception, a holy day of obligation. No school when I was a kid at St. John's. Since my birthday was the next day, my gift every year since the fifth grade was a new pair of Converse shoes for the basketball season. I walked down to Repp's Sporting Goods after mass and bought them. No Air Anybody's, just moved up from black ones to white ones.

The Supreme Court refuses to hear Trump allies' suit overturning Pennsylvania's election results. A great way to end this debacle! Maybe, just maybe, the Court shapes the justices more than the beliefs they bring with them. It has happened in the past and I continue to believe it will in the future.

December 9, 2020

DAY 265

My journal journey ends with this 290th entry since January 27. The quarantine goes on and we await our turn for the vaccine. My children bought me a beautiful leather chair for my office. Joyce is preparing a terrific birthday dinner for me. She is calling me now. I am "borrowing" my beloved Leonardo's last written line: "Perche la minestra si fredda!"